"In *Narcas*, Deborah Bonello bypasses the typical macho narco narrative into something far more complex and fascinating: a look at the powerful patronas of organized crime. Finally, we get the other half of the story in this deeply reported and masterfully written book about women who built and ran their own drug empires, no matter the cost."

—MELISSA DEL BOSQUE, author of *Bloodlines: The True Story of a Drug Cartel, the FBI, and the Battle for a Horse-Racing Dynasty*

"Deborah Bonello, a renowned journalist and author, brilliantly captures the ascension of women into leadership roles within the dark, violent world of powerful drug cartels dominated by ruthless men for many decades."

—MIKE VIGIL, former DEA chief of international operations

"This incredibly well-researched and well-written book approaches the world of drug trafficking in a unique and novel fashion—through the eyes and stories of the women who live and work in that world. By telling the stories of these women, the book debunks the long-standing view that narcas are simply eye candy or accessories for their men and shows that smart, aggressive women can be leaders in their own right. An excellent piece of investigative journalism!"

—BONNIE S. KLAPPER, criminal defense attorney and former federal prosecutor

"Deborah Bonello has years of experience in Mexico and the smarts to probe deep—and it shows in *Narcas*. From El Chapo's young wife to the women and girls enduring misogyny in Central America's gangs, this is a fascinating narrative, a behind-the-scenes look at an aspect of the drug business most people don't know about."

—TRACY WILKINSON, senior foreign policy writer and former Latin America bureau chief for the *Los Angeles Times*

"In a feat of intrepid reporting, Deborah Bonello travels to the front lines of the cartel wars to uncover stories of women who have risen through the ranks. *Narcas* is an important and nuanced corrective to decades of blinkered reporting on the drug trade—and essential reading for anyone who really wants to understand the culture within it."

—EVAN RATLIFF, cofounder of the *Longform* podcast
and author of *The Mastermind: A True Story
of Murder, Empire, and a New Kind of Crime Lord*

NARCAS

THE
SECRET RISE OF
WOMEN
IN LATIN AMERICA'S
CARTELS

DEBORAH BONELLO

BEACON PRESS
BOSTON

Beacon Press
Boston, Massachusetts
www.beacon.org

Beacon Press books
are published under the auspices of
the Unitarian Universalist Association of Congregations.

26 25 24 23   8 7 6 5 4 3 2 1

This book is printed on acid-free paper that meets the uncoated paper
ANSI/NISO specifications for permanence as revised in 1992.

Text design and composition by Kim Arney

Library of Congress Cataloguing-in-Publication
Data is available for this title.
Hardcover ISBN: 978-0-8070-0704-4
E-book ISBN: 978-0-8070-0705-1
audiobook: 978-0-8070-1279-6

CONTENTS

AUTHOR'S NOTE

The research for this book was based on a hunch as well as, if I'm honest, a grudge, about the way that women are represented in organized crime. Both the hunch and the grudge paid off, and most of my research is based on three main reporting sources: interviews with women—and men—from the criminal world, as well as experts and law enforcement; court documents outlining cases in the US justice system; and, finally, third-party reports and government statistics when I could find them.

I can't claim that my methods are terribly scientific compared to those used in academic research, and there was more of an emphasis on qualitative rather than quantitative data. The combination of both types of findings did confirm to me that my hunch—that there are many more women in many more leadership roles in organized crime than most of the existing mainstream literature and coverage would have us believe—was correct. My findings go way beyond the anecdotal.

I make no apologies for this—I am a journalist, not a social scientist or statistician. My purpose in writing this book was to create compelling stories and new narratives, as well as share my own stories and experiences, in a field where old-school gender tropes still dominate.

Due to the nature of the reporting, many of the determining characteristics and names of people I interviewed have been changed or withheld to keep them safe when the book comes out. It's a compromise I am always willing to make for those willing to share their stories and experiences with me, and I hope that you will trust me enough to relay their stories fairly and accurately without always shining a light on who they are.

INTRODUCTION

Standing alone at the front of a Chicago courtroom, Guadalupe Fernández Valencia wore orange prison coveralls. Her long light-brown hair, streaked with gray, was pulled back into a tight ponytail at the nape of her neck. She wore no makeup. She was sixty years old.

"I want to take advantage of this opportunity to ask forgiveness from my children and from my family," said Guadalupe. It was August 2021, and she was about to be sentenced for a sobering litany of drug trafficking charges, including conspiracy to transport and distribute, and money laundering.[1]

Guadalupe spent more than three decades in the drug business, working for Joaquín "El Chapo" Guzmán, the world's most famous drug lord, and his Sinaloa Cartel. She is, to date, the highest-ranking female Sinaloa Cartel operative to emerge into the public eye.

When El Chapo was convicted by a court in New York in February 2019, it was the climax of the highest-profile organized crime case of my generation. During his trial, news reporters had to arrive at three or four in the morning to get a seat for the day. El Chapo's adventures—and those of other male traffickers—have inspired Hollywood movies, Netflix series, and countless books and novels. Few women have.

So when I looked at the indictment that sent El Chapo down, an indictment on which Guadalupe was the only woman, I was struck by how unknown her story is to the world. Some superficial Googling revealed coverage of the guilty plea she made and not much else. In the history of the drug trade, public focus is nearly always on the male protagonists.

Yet Guadalupe, known as "La Patrona" (a Spanish term for a female boss), had a criminal career that ran parallel to that of El Chapo. She was arrested in Mexico just a month after his final capture.

I wondered, as she awaited her sentence in the dock, if she had calmed herself by picturing the green mountains and remembering the soft air of home. The smell of woodsmoke in the mornings. Did memories of Michoacán, the humid southern Mexican state where she was born, soothe her in that difficult moment? Any happy childhood memories had no doubt been sullied when the crime lords moved into her home state when she was a teenager. They plundered the heroin poppy and marijuana plantations in the picturesque mountains, holding humble farmers to ransom by controlling the price for poppy paste that the farmers had no choice but to accept. Those who spoke up in self-defense were either silenced or co-opted.

Eventually, the drug gangs took over entire villages like hers, often abusing the communities' younger women. They would grow to dominate not just the lucrative production of heroin and crystal meth but the mineral and gold mines dotted around the state, as well as the avocado and lime industries.

Guadalupe escaped them for a time by coming to the United States, like millions of her countrymen and women before her. But now here she was—one of them. The bosses she had worked for fronted a billion-dollar multinational operation that had tentacles reaching around the globe. They didn't just dominate a single Mexican state. They were the biggest criminal organization in the world.

"I wish I could find the words to convince you of how sorry I am," Guadalupe told Judge Sharon Johnson Coleman in court in Chicago. She was handed down a ten-year sentence, seven years of which she had already served.

But El Chapo got life. Some of the "substantial" evidence, according to US prosecutors, that eventually put him behind bars after a criminal career spanning more than four decades, came from Guadalupe.[2]

During her time working with the Sinaloa Cartel, Guadalupe worked closely with Jesús Alfredo Guzmán Salazar, known as Alfredillo, one of El Chapo's sons.[3] His name is on the same charge sheet as both Guadalupe's and his father's, but he remains at large in Mexico. Court documents describe Guadalupe as Jesús's "lieutenant." They worked together on the entire drug distribution process, from start to finish, and she was a fundamental part of the organization, prosecutors say.[4] Her crucial role in the cartel makes it even more interesting that she is so unknown. When I, a dedicated narco nerd, first learned about her, my curiosity was piqued.

By then, I had been reporting from Latin America for more than a decade, with my main focus on organized crime. I had become part of a growing group of women who are documenting the drug trade, its dynamics and its protagonists. A lot of the coverage of narco issues in general has been dominated by male writers and macho narratives. The way these stories have been told—men as victimizers and women as victims—feels excessively based on gender tropes. When Guadalupe Fernández Valencia's story inspired the idea for this book, I had a hunch that this way of viewing the trade was so one-dimensional that it was untrue, but I knew that I had to dig deeper to prove it. I wasn't interested in finding female versions of the male *cabrones* (hard macho bastards) that we constantly see in media representations of the cartels. Rather, I wanted to understand how women's power manifests in this context beyond its juxtaposition with men's.

On a visit to the Mob Museum in Las Vegas to give a talk on the investigative work for this book in June 2022, I stood in front of a wall adorned with the faces of the "100 Years of Made Men and Their Associates." There must have been a hundred men and just four women hanging on that wall. It was a stunning reminder of how broadly invisible female faces have been in organized crime over the years. Friends of mine who have written books about the drug trade have told me unabashedly that there are barely any women in their work, admitting that they might have missed something there. I remember being told on numerous occasions in the field, while covering some of the violence waged on communities by drug cartels—a few of them while I was quite pregnant—that I should probably be at home.

Now seems the right time to talk about the real, gritty, unexpected part women play in organized crime. Characters such as Wendy Byrde, Ruth Langmore, and Darlene Snell in the Netflix series *Ozark* and Polly Gray in *Peaky Blinders* are changing the narratives about women working in criminal businesses, adding nuance and color that contradict clichés. Women such as Megan Rapinoe have emerged in traditionally male sports as icons and advocates.

All of these dynamics feel connected to what I've discovered about women in the ranks of organized crime. Most of the women who have been visible in the drug trade are highly sexualized narco wives or girlfriends. The little coverage they have received tends to focus on their sexual attractiveness and attachments to male narcos, rather than their business power, the message being that if they're not attractive, they don't warrant investigation or attention.

Emma Coronel, Guzmán's much younger, infinitely more glamorous wife, epitomizes this dynamic. She was a constant presence at her husband's trial and also appeared on VH1's *Cartel Crew*, where she chatted with the family members of other drug traffickers over glasses of champagne about how to create a brand from her husband's criminal legacy. She was eventually taken into custody on a visit to Washington, DC, in early 2021.

Prosecutors alleged that she was part of a plan to break her husband out of prison for a third time before he was extradited to the United States to face trial. They also claimed that she knew about his drug trafficking activities and the origin of the proceeds. She was an enabler, the classic gangster's moll. Emma eventually turned herself in and was given a relatively light sentence despite her alleged offenses.[5]

The romantic or family attachments of women in the drug trade are often used to minimize or marginalize them as protagonists. Emma's role as El Chapo's wife is a great example. The logic seems to be that women are there because they are someone's wife or lover or sister or daughter. But men also enter the trade by virtue of their family connections—most organized crime business is also family business—and yet their influence is assumed to be larger or more important, a virtue of their maleness rather than their familial connections. Those blood or love ties are never used to explain and minimize their presence in the way they are for women.

Then there are the other women most visible in organized crime: the victims. Impoverished single mothers obliged to sell or smuggle drugs to support their families, or women coerced to entrap and kill. Women trafficked into undesirable trades. Prisons across the region are home to thousands of women like this, who are serving long sentences for relatively small crimes.

But within the binary of characterizing narco women as either wives or victims, I started to see so much more. I saw women as protagonists and decision-makers in the criminal underworld and the drug trade. I saw them in roles in which their romantic or family connections were a sidebar. Women like Guadalupe and the other protagonists in this book. Women in gangs in Central America. Women operating extortion rackets. Women involved in *narcomenudeo* (street-level drug crime). Across Latin America, the female population behind bars for offenses related to organized crime has doubled in the last decade. In Mexico and Colombia—major drug trade hubs in the region—the increase in female prisoners has been especially high.[6]

I began to wonder if women were somehow becoming more empowered in the shadows of the drug trade, even within a regional culture that does its best to hold them down. Maybe some of them see a chance to rise through a hierarchy, despite the murky morality of the drug business. Maybe women in organized crime are rising up to give orders instead of just taking them. I also wondered if the trends I was seeing were new—or if media coverage of the drug trade has just been unable, or unwilling, to see them.

I know from my reporting that the context of women's involvement in the Latin American drug trade has been changing, in pace with the growing participation of women in economic and social life. Some women see an opportunity to participate in criminal activities as a way to a potential career, the promise of money, power, influence, and status. For many women in the region, the obstacles to professional success remain daunting. Some of the women that I profile in this book come from humble, impoverished backgrounds. That they had to break the law to achieve their career goals reflects many things—from their own personality characteristics to their limited array of options for advancement and power in the mainstream professional sphere.

But to view their role as a simple reflection of necessity is to rob women of their agency, reducing them to mere pawns in a man's game. The patriarchy of the cartels seems very real, but to assume women don't have a capacity for violence or a thirst for power and status is just another narrow gender stereotype that grossly misunderstands and underestimates women and their role in the social order.

———

"Brenda" was serving a fifty-year sentence when we met in the Pavón prison in Guatemala City. She told me she enjoyed running a kidnapping ring that eventually landed her behind bars. She assured me that she didn't have to get involved in the criminal enterprise out of economic need. Her husband was a drug transporter before he was killed, leaving her plenty of money to care for herself and their three children.

"It was curiosity," she said. "I wanted to know how it felt. I wanted to feel that my life was at risk. I liked the danger."[7]

When we talked, she was fifty-four years old and twenty years into her prison term. She was hoping to get out within the next five years for good behavior.

One of Brenda's fellow inmates in Pavón also spoke to me. Her story was very different. Gloria, age forty-six, told me that one day a man brought an elderly blindfolded woman to her house, where she rented out rooms. He paid for a room for the woman, who he said was his mother-in-law, and asked Gloria to look after her. The "son-in-law" told Gloria that the woman had recently undergone eye surgery. Gloria fed and bathed the woman, who never took off the blindfold.

Within days, the police came knocking. They rescued what turned out to be a human hostage and accused Gloria of kidnapping.

"I used to bathe her and feed her, but she never told me anything, because she thought I was one of them," said Gloria, who claimed she had no idea her guest was a hostage.[8]

Gloria's story fits the stereotype of women who can be tricked or forced into organized crime by men. But Brenda's story feels equally striking and real—and like a new narrative. Brenda was owning her decision to get into kidnapping—she wasn't telling herself or anyone else that she had no choice. "I think that most of us here know what we were doing," she said about the women in prison with her. "I've never blamed anyone but myself. I own my bad acts."

Then there was Maria, whom I met via a mutual friend in the working-class barrio of Tepito, Mexico City. As we spoke, men in a nearby open-air gym lifted weights and showed off their muscles to each other.

Maria told me she began trafficking weapons as a young woman. One day, her mother, the boss of their gunrunning enterprise, was sick and couldn't make the drive to pick up guns that had been bought in the US and were being smuggled over the border to Mexico. So she sent Maria, who said she has now been selling weapons to the cartels as well as to local residents for the better part of twenty years. She's grooming her sixteen-year-old daughter to do the same.[9]

"I loved the adrenaline. I loved looking over my shoulder," Maria told me about the first time she went to pick up weapons in the northern state of Tamaulipas, across the border from Texas. Her son, she said, wasn't keen on joining the matriarchal network of gunrunners.

———

Early on a Sunday morning in May 2021, Abel Jacobo Miller took me to the outskirts of the city of Culiacán, the capital of Sinaloa, in the already searing sun. He put a Glock pistol in my hand and told me to shoot. As someone who grew up in the UK, where most guns are illegal for most people, I had never fired a weapon. When I did, my arms and hands trembled under the force of the discharge. But I knew that the more I did it, the better I would get.

The ubiquity of firearms as the weapon of choice in the criminal underworld has contributed to a leveling of the playing field for the sexes. Battles are rarely fought with fists but with military weaponry and skills that can be mastered equally by all genders. "A sixty-kilo [132-pound] woman can't confront a ninety-kilo [198-pound] man with her fists. But with a gun, with a gun we're equals," said Jacobo Miller, who teaches women self-defense and shooting in his home city. He was addressing the other women on the shooting range that day, who seemed able to handle a gun a lot better than I did.[10]

"I work with them to remove the chip that [tells them] they're vulnerable. That they're victims," the father of three daughters told me later. "Women are as threatening as men. They just have to understand that about themselves."[11]

One of the women under his tutelage that day was forty-five-year-old accountant Tessa, a lifelong resident of Culiacán. It was the first time she had fired a gun too. "It felt good," she told me. "At first, I was nervous about what it would feel like in my body, but then it felt good to shoot, and it got easier and easier.[12]

"I wanted to have the confidence to do it," she said. "With things the way they are, with so much violence, there's no room for terror. Now, it's about security and keeping us safe."

On my reporting trips over the last decade, investigating everything from gang violence and extortion to the fentanyl trade, it has become increasingly common to have women sitting across from me during interviews. And their stories are incredibly nuanced. Women are stepping around the frontiers of gender expectations to establish their own place in organized crime, one of their own making. I learned from US prosecutors who have charged women in the drug trade and from lawyers who have defended them that women often use the shroud of gender stereotypes to go undetected. Women are hiding behind the stereotype of the good girl incapable of doing bad to do just that. They become drug transporters, money launderers, and killers. Street drug vendors and packers. Weapons traffickers. Kidnappers. Extortionists.

Many of the women I've interviewed are also current or former law enforcement officers or elected officials. Both of those types of actors can be fundamental enablers of drug trafficking groups and organized crime across Latin America, even when they may appear to be fighting the illegal narcotics business. They're involved in a spectrum of ways, from taking bribes for protecting and enabling criminal actors to taxing drug traffickers for operating in their territory. In every single country in Latin America, officials at all levels collude with the drug trade. For the women featured in this book, relationships with powerful officials were a a fundamental aspect of their drug trafficking operations and the organizations they work with.

There are some commonalities among the patronas whom I document here. Most of them came into the drug business later in life. Their organizations are often clan-based, involving husbands, children, cousins, and other members of the extended family. Many come from poor backgrounds and have little formal education and few legal job opportunities. Some grew up in violent circumstances and were often violent actors themselves. As participants in the drug trade, if they are not doing the killing, they have others to do it for them. And many of them enjoy the power and thrill that the business affords.

Crucially, these women are connected to each other. Some of them have personal relationships, often working together to traffic drugs and move the cash proceeds. Others are linked because of relationships between the organizations they work for. And the more I looked, the more women I found working within the ranks of organized crime. Like men, they are present at all parts of the chain. But contemporary research on women's role in the drug trade is woefully lacking. I often wonder if this reflects a particular lens through which many of those documenting organized crime view the subject, both in academia and in the media. Most of them are men, and I wonder, do they pay more attention to the men in the room as a virtue of their own reporting biases? When they don't ask about women and their role in the drug trade, it suggests they're assuming that role is minimal. Through this lens, drug traffickers are, by definition, male. Pablo Escobar. El Chapo. John Gotti. Al Capone.

As I researched Guadalupe's life and the court case that ended with her prison sentence, I found that the role she played certainly bore a resemblance more to what are traditionally male decision-making roles in the drug trade, rather than to the role played by women like Chapo's wife, Emma Coronel. The lack of media attention on her and her criminal life didn't reflect her lack of importance or power within the Sinaloa Cartel, but instead her failure to fulfill the gender stereotypes at work in the drug trade. By the time she was detained, she was in her late fifties, and she didn't tick the "babe" or "victim" boxes that the spotlight seems to demand from women in the business.

It's true that Guadalupe may have started out as a victim. I learned about her five children and the husband who fathered them, a man who is referred to as abusive in court documents. According to her criminal lawyer, Ruben Oliva, "Over the course of her life she has had the great misfortune of . . . crossing paths with men who have only seen her as a means to an end."[13] But by the time I began reading about her, she had already served nearly ten years in an American prison after being convicted in California for drug dealing back in the late 1990s. The case I was researching wasn't her first rodeo—she knew what she was doing when she got involved with the Sinaloans.

As I researched women in the drug trade, it became increasingly obvious that there were many women involved who, like Guadalupe, did not fit the accepted tropes. High-ranking, powerful, and some-times violent women in drug organizations were not a novelty or an exception.

El Chapo's Sinaloa Cartel, born out of the Guadalajara Cartel in the late 1980s, started out moving cocaine up from producers in Colombia, Bolivia, and Peru to Mexico and over the border into the United States, alongside tons of weed and heroin. Nowadays these drugs have been joined by large quantities of methamphetamine and

fentanyl. The Sinaloans defined the modus operandi for the prolif-
eration of trafficking groups that thrive today: clandestine landing
strips in the jungle that accommodate small planes packed to the roof
with product; speedboats filled with dope ripping up the seas; drugs
disguised as other goods concealed in container trucks and cars. El
Chapo famously attempted to ship half a million dollars' worth of
cocaine into the United States from Mexico packed in jalapeño cans.[14]

The drug trafficking world and its culture has been documented
and portrayed as viscerally male and patriarchal. The ostentatious use
of brutal violence has become a defining feature of Mexico's crime
wars, as has the sexual objectification of women by elements of narco
culture such as *narcoccorido* (a genre of ballads and songs dedicated to
drug lords) and plastic surgery. Women are accessories, another sign
of male success. Emma Coronel, Chapo's wife, has come to exemplify
an aspiration lifestyle and a "look" for women involved with drug
traffickers in Culiacán, who are known as *buchonas*.[15]

The macho nature of the drug trade and its surrounding culture
also serves to hide women from view. In Honduras, the violent Valle
family drug trafficking organization was for years controlled in part by
one of our protagonists, Digna Valle. A former local government official in Honduras told me that Digna's brothers, who worked alongside
her, tried to hide her power for fear it would make them seem weak
in the context of a male-dominated culture. "Really, for the Valles,
the people at the front were Arnulfo Valle and Luis Valle [Digna's
younger brothers], but they made sure Digna Valle never appeared
to be a major protagonist in media coverage here. Later it was shown
that it was she who managed their finances and was the brain behind
a lot of their operations," said the official, whom I spoke to in Santa
Rosa de Copán.[16] The small city is close to Honduras's border with
Guatemala, which makes up a major part of the cocaine smuggling
route from south to north and the Valle's former domain.

"Digna's brothers [Luis and Arnulfo] were dedicated to sowing
fear and terror here in this region, and in this northern region in
general," said the former official. "It was only when [Digna] was

captured and taken to the United States that it started to come out how powerful she had been within the organization."[17]

Some argue that there is a fundamental difference between how men and women behave in the crime business. "There's not going to be a show and a gunfight—they [women] don't need to make a show of it like [male] cartel leaders have done in the past," criminologist Mónica Ramírez Cano told me. Cano has interviewed dozens of notorious figures from Mexico's criminal underworld, both male and female. She profiled El Chapo after his final capture in Mexico and before he was extradited to the United States.[18]

But some criminal lawyers who have defended female drug bosses in the US disagree with Cano. They told me that women crave fame and power in the drug world as much as men do.

I have found that both claims are true.

———

Guadalupe's relatively light sentence means that by the time you're reading this, it won't be long before she is released from prison. But she's unlikely to want to go home. Her former captain, El Chapo's son Jesús, aka Alfredillo, remains at large south of the border. Alongside the Guzmáns, there are six other men named in the indictment who are no doubt displeased by her cooperation with US prosecutors. One of them, Ismael "El Mayo" Zambada, cofounder of the Sinaloa Cartel and a legendary Mexican trafficker, has never set foot in a jail cell and is one of the most-wanted criminals on the Drug Enforcement Administration (DEA) radar.

Guadalupe has already said too much. If she manages to avoid deportation—which is usually the next step authorities take against foreign drug offenders like her—and remains in the US after she leaves prison, she will have to spend the rest of her life looking over her shoulder. She will have to blend in and become invisible to survive.

I'm fascinated by Guadalupe and all of the other women featured in this book. As a journalist and writer, I do my best to tread the fine line between describing their exploits and the complexities of their stories without celebrating their criminal achievements. As a woman surrounded mostly by men investigating organized crime, I'm used to seeing women either underestimated or ignored. And that feels like an attitude shaped more by gender stereotypes and assumptions than by facts. Overlooking women is a mistake, and these women's stories prove that.

To be clear, this book is not about finding the female version of El Chapo, because that would be trying to squeeze women into a male trope. The challenge is to identify and recognize women's power for what it is within the context of organized crime. The power they wield is often not the same as that of men, but we need to see it if we're to better understand the criminal shadows in which they move.

CHAPTER I

THE MATRIARCH

THE FIEFDOM

The tiny town of El Espíritu sits at the end of a long red-dirt road, nestled in the lush green mountains of northwest Honduras. To the untrained eye, it looks just like one of the tens of thousands of *pueblitos* (little towns) scattered across Latin America: a small central plaza fronted by a church; unpaved streets with litter embedded in the mud; kids wandering around barefoot; laundry hanging outside small modest houses; corner shops selling household basics and Coca-Cola.

But outsiders can only visit El Espíritu with permission from a handful of the three thousand or so residents. Or they must be accompanied by a trusted local contact. For this was once the bastion of one of the country's most violent and powerful drug trafficking clans and their matriarch, Digna Valle. She and her clan ran the town like their own personal fiefdom. The shadow of the Valles family's reign still lies over the town.

Digna was arrested when she arrived in Miami in 2014 on a business trip. She had flown from Honduras to the US not knowing that a sealed federal indictment against her and two of her brothers, Luis Alonso and Miguel Arnulfo, the result of years of investigative work by the DEA, awaited her. It was in part thanks to her that the American government was able to bring down her drug trafficking family, as well as others in the business. She was the first domino to fall, and I guess she talked. Seven years isn't a long sentence for the cocaine conspiracy charges for which she was convicted. She is now in her early sixties and at the time of writing was living in Houston after being released from prison in 2018.

As my guide—Monseñor (Bishop) Darwin Andino—and I drove into El Espíritu in his cream-colored pickup, he pointed out a field from behind the wheel. Some $11 million had once been unearthed there, after having been buried inside a water tank, he said. At the height of the Valles' operations in the international cocaine trade, the family was generating more cash than it knew what to do with.

I hadn't had to work too hard to convince Darwin, the bishop of Copán—the state, or department, of Honduras in which El Espíritu is located—to accompany me that day in March 2021. A few days earlier, I'd gone knocking on the door of his parish building in the small city of Santa Rosa de Copán, which is around a ninety-minute drive from El Espíritu. Before I talked to him, the whole idea of asking if he could take me to the town seemed audacious and preposterous at best and downright stupid at worst. But I kept reminding myself how the Catholic Church remains one of the few institutions that drug trafficking royalty in the region respects—over and above the government. And, luckily for me, Darwin was game for the adventure.

When we sat down around a vast mahogany table in his parish building to chat about why I was in town, he knew who Digna was. At this point, I had been investigating her for two years. To say I was a little obsessed would be fair. I had reached out to everyone who surrounded Digna's criminal and immigration cases in the US and, via some intermediaries, asked for an interview several times, but she had always declined. I figured that going to her hometown, where she was still known and respected, would help me understand more about her story. Darwin concurred.

We rumbled toward the tiny town a few days later, the pickup kicking out a cloud of red dust behind us. A couple of young children, one still in diapers, walked hand in hand along the road's edge on their way to one of the tiny one-story wooden houses that flanked the way in. It had been a hardscrabble life here for Digna, the first of thirteen siblings. The houses looked small and cramped. Fires burned in some of the front yards, and skinny chickens scraped in the dirt.

"I pray for Honduras every day," said Darwin. "The poverty here is immense. Immense."

As we approached the entrance to El Espíritu, Darwin said, "I've been told that here in this town, to go in, they used to have a lot of security guards. That they would often stop vehicles and ask, 'Who are you?' and 'Where are you going?' and then they would follow you to make sure."

But now the guards were gone, their bosses mostly behind bars in the US and Honduras. We felt eyes on us, but nobody stopped us from rolling in.

El Espíritu couldn't have been more different from the environments one might associate with the fast-paced cocaine business. It was sleepy. Quiet. Stray dogs ambled around the unpaved streets, and locals walked around in flip-flops. Any noise was that generated from radios inside houses, or the few cars and trucks rumbling through.

Digna was born in the 1960s, and by the time she was a teenager, the international cocaine business in the region was booming. Honduras soon became a major transit country for the drug, which is produced in the South American nations of Peru, Bolivia, and Colombia, and then transported north to consumers in the United States. It was in the early 2000s, when Digna was in her forties and the mother of two children, when her family got themselves, and most of the town, involved in the cocaine boom.

"Digna was one of the faithful," said Darwin as the massive Catholic Church she helped build loomed into view.

As he spoke, I thought about how Bishop Darwin was the best local guide I could have dreamed of. A lapsed Catholic myself, I made a mental note to stop trash-talking the Church.

The huge church far outweighed the spatial if not the spiritual needs of the town's tiny congregation. A well-kept concrete structure painted pale yellow, it dwarfed the other buildings in the town. Out front, a neatly cut green lawn had a paved esplanade at its center that was punctuated with white benches. The back of the first bench Darwin and I strolled to was embossed with the words "DIGNA ASUSENA VALLE Y FAMILIA." Next to that was another bench: "LUIS VALLE, MAYRA LEMUS Y HIJOS." And another: "JOSE REYNERIO VALLE Y FAMILIA." And another: "REMBER CUESTAS VALLE Y FAMILIA." The church's sponsors.

Digna is a woman of contradictions. As a resident of El Espíritu, she took great pride in her social acts, such as the quality and size of the church and the café ranches—coffee farms—that she helped fund and run as part of a portfolio of family businesses. Residents told me she used to ride out to the ranches dressed "like a man" in trousers with a hat on, then get off the horse to sit down and eat lunch with the workers. She also oversaw the organization of parties for local religious festivals and used family money to put on a spread to make sure everyone in the town enjoyed themselves.

But there was a darker side to Digna that emerged as pressure on her family began to grow and the US government leaned more and more on its Honduran allies to bring in the Valle Cartel and cut off their trafficking business.

ATTENTION TO DETAIL

After visiting the church, Darwin and I got back into the pickup and continued through town. As we crawled slowly along the main dirt road, visual nuances spoke to the town's history. Near El Espíritu's entrance was what had the makings of a large mansion. The gray raw concrete walls were two floors high, and they curled around a huge courtyard with what looked like the beginnings of a swimming pool at its center. Such a construction would have been well beyond the means of the average family here in Copán, who relied on local jobs such as coffee farming.

It was apparent that the work on the building had been abandoned years ago. A fence covered in weeds and vines partially obscured the gray monolith. Long grass was thriving where the pool was planned, and the holes where the windows would have been gaped like open mouths gasping for air. Digna, locals told me, had been building the mansion for herself and her husband and adult children, Gerson and Tesla, until her arrest forced construction to a sudden stop.

I was told by both those close to her and locals of the area that Digna was the "good face" of the Valle family, loved and respected by the community. The eldest of thirteen brothers and sisters, she was "the mother of them all," said one local resident, who asked to be called Teresa and who had lived in the area for more than two decades. Teresa had socialized and worked alongside the family during their years of dominance, which began in the late 1990s. "I liked her. She looked like a *trabajadora* [a hard-working woman]. She was made of brute force," Teresa told me when we met in Santa Rosa de Copán. "She was sociable but of strong character."

In towns like El Espíritu, the state is almost completely absent, and Digna represented an authority, an unofficial benefactor who had received very little formal education. People gathered around her because she gave them a sense of security, as well as jobs and support. She and her family were the providers and the law, both feared and respected. Looking at the girth of the mansion Digna had begun to build, I tried to reconcile it with locals' descriptions of her as humble and generous. Had she lost her sense of humility as the power of her clan increased and pressure on its operations grew? In the early 2000s, the US administration relied on its law enforcement partners in the Honduran government to dismantle the Valle clan, among others, hoping (unrealistically) to cut off the cocaine gush. At some point, Digna's community spirit likely gave way to the need to survive and take care of her own.

"They were millionaires, they were rich, and we were so poor," said one resident who used to live alongside the Valle family.

Ostentatious and huge, the mansion sent a message to the town's residents as well as to those who were after her: *Don't mess with us now. We're the ones in charge.*

When Digna started work on the mansion, around 2014, her family had been in the cocaine trafficking business for some twenty years. Denial must have seemed futile when she was arrested that year in Miami: she pleaded guilty to the charges. Just months after her arrest, her brothers were arrested in El Espíritu in a massive joint police operation between US and Honduran officers that has become the stuff of legend among local residents. Police and soldiers descended on the town en masse, searching houses until they found Luis Alonso and Miguel Arnulfo, who were promptly flown to the capital, Tegucigalpa, by helicopter. They were rapidly extradited to the US, subsequently convicted on drug charges, and sentenced to twenty-three years each behind bars.

Digna's mansion was far from the only one in her tiny town, which is peppered with the once-splendid houses owned by her brothers and other members of the Valle family. But now they're skeletons, ransacked by locals and claimed by the state. A Honduran soldier lounged outside one of them in a low chair as we drove by. He was in full uniform, playing with his cell phone and smoking a cigarette, his automatic weapon laid across his lap. He looked up at us as we rolled by, but he didn't get out of his seat. Darwin said that he had once counted a total of nineteen outsized houses or mansions on a previous visit to El Espíritu, all of which he guessed were former properties of the Valles.

WELCOMED

Digna is the reason this book exists. I was pointed in her direction in 2019 by a criminal lawyer who at the time was representing other women on trial for trafficking cocaine. Learning some of the details of her life prompted my interest and research into the role of women in Latin America's drug trade. But I found very little on her via the internet, other than some coverage of her arrest and the court documents related to her case. The few photos that I came across showed her from what I guessed were her mid-thirties onward: a stout, fair-skinned woman with a level gaze. Her hair was different colors in different pictures, and she clearly paid attention to its shade and style. She was pictured a few times wearing jeans and polo shirts, standing in front of different buildings in the small towns dotted around the green rural state where she grew up. Coming to El Espíritu seemed the only way to find out more about her.

Darwin and I drew to a stop in front of a modest one-story cement house painted blue. As we waited in the front room, I looked at the half-dozen framed certificates hanging on the faded blue walls. Many of them bore the name of a woman, a resident of the house, who had earned a law degree. Nearly all of the certificates had the same surname: Valle.

The certificates hanging on the wall belonged to a relative of Digna's; Digna herself never made it past a secondary school education, according to her former neighbors. For women of her generation, education was not seen as a priority. For her to have eventually accrued such wealth must have exceeded her life expectations tremendously. It was understandable that she wanted to show that off with elaborate houses and noble gestures.

Darwin's contact, Juanita, came into the room, and we introduced ourselves. Then Juanita insisted that we meet her mother. We quickly left her place and struggled up a steep gravel hill. On the way, we passed an enormous bright-turquoise Evangelical Christian temple, so big it looked as though it could house the town's entire population.

"Luis built that," said Juanita.[1] The structure was as big as the Catholic Church at the heart of the town.

Luis Alonso Valle and Miguel Arnulfo Valle, two of Digna's brothers, were the violent muscle behind the Valle Cartel. Just a few months before Luis Alonso's extradition to the US, in early 2014, he had been arrested by the local police in El Espíritu for allegedly raping a young girl. He was held in Santa Rosa de Copán, according to press reports and locals. At that point his fame as a drug boss was well-established and fear of him ingrained in the community. Miguel Arnulfo reportedly came to his brother's rescue, surrounding the town with armed henchman and threatening war if Luis Alonso wasn't freed. The local authorities, in turn, summoned the armed forces: "They called in the army because [Miguel] Arnulfo arrived with an AR-15 mounted on a truck," said a former Santa Rosa de Copán official, who asked me not to use his name.[2]

But after a tense standoff, the government forces were ordered to stand down, and Luis Alonso was promptly released, witnesses and locals told me. It's possible that the size and weaponry of his criminal army outdid that of the government—a dynamic common around Latin America. The family of the underaged girl who was allegedly raped was convinced to drop the charges against him.

———————

As we reached the house of Juanita's mother, Juanita gestured to the adjacent residence. "Digna lived next door to us," she said.

I stopped walking and stared at the tiny single-story mustard-yellow house topped with a corrugated roof. Digna had never gotten to live in the mansion she'd been building before she was arrested. She spent her last days in El Espíritu in this functional, pretty but humble home. This house was notably untouched compared to her brothers' palatial mansions, now in the hands of the state. Digna's house was locked and, according to her neighbors, exactly how she left it.

"[Digna] was a great woman, a great woman, and a fighter. She helped us a lot, helping with the construction of the church," said Juanita. "We built it all together, making tamales and cakes." She had to shout a little over the barking of a Siberian husky that I could see through a gap in the locked garage doors of Digna's place. Someone usually comes to feed the dog, she said, but hadn't been by for a few days. The barking felt ominous, like a portent. I figured the dog was there to warn intruders to stay away.

This was the house Digna had left that day in 2014 to fly to Miami, where she was arrested. I wished that I could have been a fly on the wall back then, listening to family conversations between her, her husband, and her kids, Gerson and Tesla. Her kids couldn't have known back then that their mother would soon be arrested and that her cooperation with US agents and prosecutors would bring to an end the criminal empire they had all been building for years.

After Digna's arrest, Tesla was eventually taken into custody for money laundering. And Gerson, who went on the lam for four years after his mother and his uncles were arrested, eventually turned himself in to US authorities in Florida. Media reports in Honduras later suggested that while she was in custody, Digna was in touch with Gerson and talked him into turning himself in. It seems likely that she incriminated both of her children during her time in US detention.

In October 2013, prior to Digna's final trip to Miami, an associate paid a visit to Digna's home to discuss the transportation of two tons of cocaine scheduled to arrive on the east coast of Honduras via speedboat, the US government claimed in Digna's proffer agreement. This is how things worked, and continue to work, in Honduras. Shipments of cocaine, marijuana, and heroin are brought north by sea from Colombia and Venezuela and dropped off in a part of the country called *La Mosquitia*, in the department of Gracias a Dios, which translates as "Thanks be to God." But the only people thankful for this band of land on the Caribbean coast, which is covered in dense swamps and forests and practically impassable, are traffickers who can operate clandestinely there with little interference from the authorities.[3]

Dope is moved from the coast via improvised roads that traffickers and their associates have forged through the foliage and muck until they meet with major highways, along which they move their valuable cargo to Honduras's border with Guatemala.

Digna's family's fiefdom there on the border in Copán was *the* spot for moving cocaine into Guatemala on its way to the US. She would organize the offloading of the drugs from the Valle Cartel's partners and its safe passage into Guatemala. The US government estimates that from around 2009 until Digna's arrest in 2014, she and her family moved tens of thousands of kilos of cocaine across the Honduras-Guatemala border every month. Digna made as much as $800,000 from moving a single shipment, like the one dropped off as a result of the deal she made that October day in 2013.

NO MAN'S LAND

As the crow flies, Digna's house in El Espíritu is less than ten kilometers south of the border with Guatemala. The international line, like most of the land borders in Latin America, is porous and mostly lawless. The border police have few resources to prevent drugs from passing into Guatemala. Their one patrol car sits on the side of a road near the border. It is out of service, its two front wheels missing.[4]

What doesn't pass undetected through the few official crossing points on the Honduras-Guatemala border makes its way clandestinely between the two countries. For the fifteen or so formal entry points that exist along the entire international line, there are more than a hundred clandestine ones, many of which can be traversed by trucks along dirt roads.[5]

This sliver of Central America is considered one of the most dangerous areas in Latin America. It has one of the highest murder rates in the world.[6] That's largely because Honduras is one of the unfortunate countries to lie between Colombia, Peru, and Bolivia—the nations that produce cocaine—and the United States, the country that consumes the most cocaine in the world.[7] Operators like Digna's Valle clan corrupt local and national authorities and challenge the ability of governments to govern, leaving behind a blood-stained trail littered with dollars.

The lack of state presence on the border allows for groups like the Valle Cartel to come in and fill a void, both charming and terrorizing local communities with their own brand of criminal governance.

Social deeds such as building churches, creating jobs, and handing out loans come at a price, and the relationship between Digna and her community operated in a fine balance. The more powerful and violent the Valle clan became, the less trusted Digna was by the community she had dedicated herself to.

The Valles started as cattle rustlers and contraband smugglers, a way of life on the border that enabled families to become experts in negotiating the land and the politics in the region. As cocaine began to arrive from South America, it displaced the cows and cigarettes that the family used to smuggle into Guatemala. After a coup against the government of President Manuel Zelaya in 2009, which created even more political distractions from the activities of organized crime, the trickle of cocaine became a gush.[8]

The Valles worked with a different group to the east called the Cachiros and grew into a vital go-between for organizations operating across the region, including Joaquín "El Chapo" Guzmán's Sinaloa Cartel in Mexico.

As Digna accrued the kind of wealth that prompted her to start construction on her mega-mansion, the lines between official and de facto authorities started to blur in Copán. The Valles imposed laws as they saw fit, corrupting or co-opting state officials as a means of furthering and protecting their interests. Police became an armed wing for private, not public, interests in return for increased salaries and other perks.[9] "It is like this," a police officer on the Honduran side of the Guatemala-Honduras border told researchers:

> If you need a battery for your patrol car, you can ask headquarters and it will take six months and may never come, and then the bosses will try to make you pay for it. Or the local *señores* have someone give you a new battery, put in new brakes, fill the tank with gasoline, as long as you don't bother them. We park where they tell us to park. We look where they tell us to look. No one has any trouble.[10]

The massive Catholic church in the nearby tiny town of La Florida, which I also visited, boasts stained glass windows depicting Mother Teresa and Pope John Paul II. Green benches outside on the main zocalo, or plaza, in front of the church also bear the name of the local mayor, Rember—the same Rember whose name is inscribed on the benches in front of the church in El Espíritu. Only on this bench he left off his second surname: Valle.

As I'm writing this, Rember has been mayor of La Florida for the last nine years.[11] Digna made sure that her cousin got the votes he needed to get elected. After all, the point of spending large amounts of money locally and helping community members was to buy the loyalty of the town. For a while, it worked. When the National Police were sent from the capital, Tegucigalpa, to arrest members of the Valle family for drug crimes, the Valles would go underground, and townsfolk would tell police they didn't even know the people they were trying to arrest, much less where they might be hiding.

One former resident remembered the day their father came home and told them not to get excited about the Valles turning up at their school to hand out food and cakes. "People are saying really bad things about the Valle family now," they remembered him saying. "Everyone knew—even us young people when we were just seven or eight years old—we all knew that they were trafficking drugs," they recalled. It was around that time that Digna started to wear a wig during public events, to try to go undetected, I was told.[12] The tide was turning against the family as the US government tightened the screws on the Honduran administration to arrest them. Ultimately, US authorities had to wait for Digna to come to them to arrest her themselves.

VIKINGS

The Valles' rapid consolidation of power mutated their role: first they were benefactors and providers, but they soon became violent oppressors. When Luis Alonso was accused of raping a minor in 2014, it wasn't an isolated incident.

Former residents of Honduras who are now seeking asylum in the United States told me that Luis Alonso and his brother Miguel Arnulfo would habitually abduct young teenage girls that they took a fancy to and take them to their houses. One witness said that the brothers would "go first," and then the girls would be passed around to other members of the family and, finally, the bodyguards. After being raped by each of those men, they were eventually returned home in tatters. Their families were told that if they reported the rapes to anyone, their entire families would be killed.

"Once I was in the kitchen when locals were complaining to Digna that her brothers had taken young girls up there. And Digna said that the young girls shouldn't have gone around provoking her brothers," remembered a former resident of El Espíritu. "Doña Digna would say, 'They have to be killed. We can't leave them like that,' about families and people who knew too much or did things the family didn't like."[13]

As the years went by, Digna's community spirit eroded as she strived to protect her family and her criminal profits. If she couldn't buy the loyalty and silence of certain locals, some allege that she took it upon herself to silence them forever. The coexistence of these violent tactics and her social popularity created a strong tension around her presence in the town.

Digna was never convicted for violent crimes, and I wasn't able to verify the allegations that refugees from El Espíritu made to me. In one incident described to me, a family that had been working with US law enforcement to inform on the Valle Cartel in Copán were discovered by people loyal to the Valles. When Digna found out, she allegedly dispatched two trucks of armed men to assassinate the entire family. When the US agents handling the family were told of the approaching henchmen, they allegedly flew eleven members of the family out immediately on a government plane.

When an extract of this chapter was published in *VICE World News* in late 2021, some of the women who had welcomed me in when I visited El Espíritu were enraged. They wrote to me insisting that Digna was never a killer and that I had published lies. Conversely, people in the legal community questioned the shiny version of Digna that I was given by her former employees and fellow residents of El Espíritu.

I don't know what to believe. It's tempting to embrace the version of Digna as the "good face" of the Valle Cartel but maybe only because it fits gender stereotypes of women as peacemakers. Women would never send out hits on people, right? But receiving those messages from Digna's neighbors did not feel good. I remember walking to pick one of my kids up from school in the afternoon when the first complaint came through. I felt a cold wave go through my body when I read their displeasure at the story. Then I started to sweat as I considered the possible consequences of bad-mouthing a member of the Valle Cartel. But I still think the decision to share what I was told from all sides about Digna's character was the best one, given my limited access to her.

"She wasn't violent, but she was strong," another person who knew and loved her told me. But it's hard to see how she could have survived as a cocaine transporter and protected her café ranches and other businesses without using violence. At the same time, it's possible that her brothers took care of that side of things.

The Valle family needed more than violence to keep their drug business running. They needed the Honduran government on board to keep both the National Police and the gringos off their backs. In 2013, another high-level meeting took place near El Espíritu. The men at that table were all heavily armed. They included El Chapo; Antonio "Tony" Hernández, the brother of the future Honduran president Juan Orlando Hernández, who at that moment was planning his presidential campaign; and Amilcar Alexander Ardón Soriano, who was the mayor of the nearby town of El Paraíso. It's unclear if Digna was at that table, on which sat a mound of cash, but her family interests certainly were represented there.

The money on the table in front of them amounted to a million dollars. "We counted it," Ardón later said in a court in Manhattan. "It was in plastic bags." The money was a "donation" to the political campaign of Tony's brother, Juan Orlando, from Digna's family and

El Chapo. Juan Orlando Hernández went on to win the presidency in the election in November that year. In return for the million bucks, the soon-to-be president allegedly agreed to provide protection for the drug smuggling activities of Guzmán, Ardón, and Digna's family.[14]

At the time, Chapo was on one of his visits to El Espíritu. Locals and investigators told me that he was something of a regular in the area, especially during the thirteen years he was on the lam after his first escape from a maximum-security prison in Mexico in 2001. Until he was recaptured in 2014, he sometimes enjoyed the Valle hospitality in El Espíritu, including, allegedly, partying to the tunes of Los Tigres del Norte, the world-famous ranchero band that the Valles flew in. The band did not reply to my requests to verify these allegations.

Locals knew when one of El Chapo's visits was imminent, because security in the town would increase, and the residents' movement was restricted. One resident told me that brand-new sparkling trucks would come into the village and drive down the main street on the way to the Valle residences. "That's when we knew that the real bosses were in town. We would tremble all the way down to our feet."[15]

Our guide in El Espíritu, Juanita, remembered, "When [the Valles] were still here, there were parties, and they paid for everything. A lot of people would come down from the mountains, and the cars would be lined up. People would come from all over the place."

But months later, Digna's arrest in Miami showed that the million-dollar deal Chapo had arranged with Honduran officials that day protected the Valles from nothing. When the DEA nabbed Digna, the Valle brothers were enraged, and they wanted revenge. They put out a hit on the president of Honduras, Juan Orlando Hernández, for having reneged on his promise to protect them.

US law enforcement, which had been working closely with its counterparts in Honduras, saw the hit coming and learned that the Valles were being aided by the fellow signatory on the deal: El Chapo. The gunmen were arrested before they could carry out the hit on Hernández. Miguel Arnulfo and Luis Alonso were also detained and subsequently extradited.

"Tony Hernández told me that the Valles had been captured because they had tried to kill the president of Honduras," said Ardón in court.[16]

Former president Hernández has always denied any connection to the drug trade, even as the testimony of Honduran drug lords against him mounted in the US courts. He issued a virulent denial of the guilt of his brother Tony when he was sentenced to life in prison for his role in the drug trade in March 2021. But former president Hernández's version of events—that the region's biggest drug lords, now in the US justice system, conspired to construct a false but convincing narrative implicating both Tony and himself—didn't convince prosecutors in the US. In early 2022, weeks after leaving office, Hernández was indicted in the Southern District Court of New York on drug trafficking charges.[17] He was extradited weeks later.

I cannot say how much Digna's cooperation with US law enforcement during her time in custody had to do with the charges that were eventually brought against former President Hernández. But her own brothers Luis Alonso and Miguel Arnulfo are both mentioned as criminal associates of Hernández's in the charge sheet against him—information that could have come from them as well as Digna.

Despite the evidence against Digna and her family, many of those in El Espíritu insisted that she was an innocent bystander. "I can't say that Digna was involved in drug trafficking. She never lived in a lot of luxury, she didn't dress fancy, I never saw that," said Juanita, standing outside Digna's modest house. The dog was still barking inside. The half-constructed mansion across town as well as a jury in Florida suggested that Juanita was either mistaken or lying.

At the end of her prison time in the United States, another legal battle was brewing for Digna. It's standard practice for foreign-national offenders who have committed aggravated felonies or drug trafficking crimes to be deported to their home countries after doing their time. Often they are deported regardless of the assistance they may have provided in incriminating others and the dangers they might face when they're sent home. Reporting on Digna's situation at the time of her release, I was struck by how the American government was effectively preparing to throw her to the wolves despite the help she'd given to prosecutors during her time in custody. I felt compassion for her. It seemed unfair to send her to certain death, given her efforts to make up for her past offenses.

"It's a death sentence for her," Mike Vigil, former chief of international operations at the DEA, told me at the time I was reporting her story: "Her chances of survival in Honduras are slim to none. Honduras is, without question, a narco state. The highest levels within the political spectrum, along with the military and police, are in the pockets of drug traffickers. Given the fact that she cooperated in key drug trafficking trials, she is not likely to survive in Honduras. She is going into a fiery cauldron and is definitely going to get burned."[18]

Whistleblower and former Honduran Army captain Santos Rodríguez Orellana also emphasized the danger Digna faced if sent home: "There is a hunt right now in my country for people who collaborated and then cooperated [with law enforcement] in drug trafficking cases."[19] He was suspended from his role in the army in 2014 after calling for an investigation into whether a helicopter used to traffic drugs was connected to powerful political elites. Namely the president's own brother, Tony, who is now doing life in a US prison for his role in the cocaine trade.

When I was writing about Digna's possible deportation, she didn't want to talk to me. She was eventually given the right to stay in the United States under the United Nations Convention Against Torture. By the time that I made the pilgrimage to El Espíritu, sources told me that she was living in Houston, Texas, after finally being released by US Immigration and Customs Enforcement (ICE).

"But does she want to come home, despite the dangers?" I asked Juanita as we entered her mother's house in El Espíritu.

I would be able to ask Digna myself.

As we came through the door, a woman walked out from the back room with her cell phone extended in her hand. "Do you want to talk to Doña Digna?" she asked me. On the phone screen, I could see a woman sitting on the edge of a bed. She was looking right back at me. It was Digna.

I froze. I had not, even in my wildest dreams, expected to speak to her face to face while in El Espíritu. My mind suddenly began working at a hundred kilometers a second. I had described myself to Juanita and her mother as a writer, not a journalist. Would Digna figure out that I was the same person she had twice denied an interview? Would she be furious that I was sitting in the house next door to hers, in her hometown in the middle of nowhere that she missed so desperately? Did she still have a button that she could press to send the heavies round? Were the women I was surrounded by part of her inner cadre? All of this raced through my mind as I smiled into the camera and tried to remain calm.

"Everybody's there," said Digna as the phone was moved around the house to show everyone sitting in the living room, including Bishop Darwin; my local journalist colleague; and my driver, a former law enforcement official who had already survived a number of attempts on his life. Digna spoke slowly, and her voice betrayed her age. She sounded weary, not like the powerhouse that residents of El Espíritu had described. The depleted appearance of the woman on the screen contrasted starkly with the depictions of a formidable, violent player in the drug business. But then, she was also smart and knew how to work people and the system, which is how she had managed to spend comparatively little time in prison compared to her brothers.

"Yes, they're here asking for you, Doña Digna," said the woman holding the phone.

I winced. We were being flagged. There was a silence as I made eye contact with my team and repressed the urge to say under my breath, "Let's get the fuck out of here."

"How are you?" Bishop Darwin asked Digna.

"Good, thanks be to God," she replied. The COVID pandemic had delayed her immigration hearing, adding to her time in detention, she said. I asked her if she was glad to be out.

"Yeah, but I don't like going outside. Everybody here says I prefer being locked indoors," she laughed.

We laughed too. Nervously.

"You're visiting?" Digna asked me and the bishop.

"Yeah, we're having a look around the town," I replied. "The town is lovely! Super pretty!"

"Ah yes, very. Did you like the church?" she asked, clearly proud of her community contribution.

"Loved it," I said. "Just sorry we didn't get to see inside."

Juanita would let us in, Digna told us, looking delighted that we'd get to see the fruits of her labor. "The details—those are my work and tastes. I hope to see you there sometime," she added.

I stopped breathing. *She's coming home?* I thought, staggered. "Are you coming home?" I asked.

"I don't know yet," said Digna after a pause. "But I think so."

"You're not afraid to come back to Honduras?" I asked, trying to hide my incredulity.

"No," she said. Ovaries of steel or bravado? There was no way of knowing.

"No?"

"No."

Conversation turned to the recent death of a close friend, the father of the family in whose house we sat. Before he died, he went to visit Digna in prison in the US. The family showed us the photos of him and Digna together, and at the mention of his name, Digna began to cry. She moved herself out of the view of the camera at her end, and soon the call was cut off. The women around us went silent for a moment, which is when it struck me that there were no men from the family left in the house. Only the women remained.

When I reflect on that trip, I am grateful that those women welcomed me into their homes. As has been so common throughout my reporting in Latin America, I have always been humbled by the dozens of families who have let me sit with them around their kitchen tables, whoever I am and whoever they are, and told me about their lives. The women of El Espíritu were no different.

Their antipathy toward me after having read some of my reporting on Digna felt uncomfortable. It didn't feel good to know that they might now regret having spoken to me about their lives. Relationships with sources are one of the most challenging parts of reporting a story like this. I was most struck by their loyalty to a matriarch who had been gone nearly a decade. They still had her back and let her know as soon as someone came around asking about her, even after so many years. Their loyalty to her didn't stop them from extending their hospitality to me.

The dynamics between women—rivalries, loyalties, influence—are invisible but powerful elements of the drug trade. I wouldn't have understood their importance in Digna's life and her role in the drug trade had I not gone to El Espíritu myself. Matriarchs like her, although so unseen, are in fact evidence of history repeating itself. Women have been movers and shakers in the narco business since the drug war began.

CHAPTER 2

NARCO WOMEN—THE STORY SO FAR

When historian Elaine Carey stepped up to the podium in Salt Lake City, Utah, in 2005, at a conference on the history of women in Mexico, she didn't know it, but she was about to make history herself. The paper she presented that day blew the minds of the hundreds of people in the audience, most of them top scholars in their field. Her study focused on María Dolores Estévez Zuleta, better known as Lola "La Chata," who was a major narcotics dealer and supplier. In the 1930s and '40s.

The audience couldn't believe what they were hearing.

"People thought I was presenting a work of fiction," remembered Carey during a conversation we had in late 2021.[1] She had written to me after hearing an interview I did with NPR about my *VICE* series *Las Patronas* on women in the drug trade, to tell me about her own book chronicling the history of women in the drug trade. After I got over the initial embarrassment of not having read her book (I had looked for books on the subject but clearly not very well), I wrote back to her, and we agreed to talk. Her research focused on the twentieth century, and mine picked up where hers left off.[2]

Carey told me that after her presentation, during the question-and-answer session, "I realized I was really on to something. The women in the trade were hiding in plain sight in newspapers, in literature, and in documents. Yet we, collectively, had missed them. I know I surprised everyone with the topic because I was looking at a woman in an earlier period and moving in a new direction. That continues to surprise, almost twenty years later, which is why the work we do is so important."[3]

When it comes to organized crime, history is rarely written by the victors, because there hardly ever are any. Despite the fame and glory that is the stuff of mafia legend, the majority of gangsters, from bosses to foot soldiers, eventually end up either dead or in prison. If and when they get out, most of them spend the rest of their lives looking over their shoulders in case old rivals come looking for them. A lucky few have the good fortune of growing old quietly under the radar.

Those who do write organized crime's history or prosecute those involved—academics, journalists, and law enforcement officials—are overwhelmingly male. Carey says, "History has minimized the role of women in organized crime. Journalists and historians who have been predominantly male loved the gangster myths, and they circulated those tales. Women are wives, mothers, sisters, and lovers but rarely seen as equal partners. They weren't all sitting at the stove stirring the sauce. Even if they were, they were listening."

An expert on gangs in Latin America, Dennis Rodgers, agrees: "The media and academia have been very guilty of basically projecting women as either being victims of the drug trade, suffering the consequences, whether it's as mothers of addicts or the suffering wives of drug dealers, or as being people who haven't been involved. And I think both of these are quite wrong."[4]

Rodgers, like Carey and I, also notes that many of the researchers in organized crime are male. This male perspective has tended to frame women within male assumptions about them, which obscures the extent of their power or roles in the drug trade. Carey believes that men's assumptions have prevented them from being able to see women as central figures at all: "The fact is that the men writing about organized crime and the drug trade never bothered to ask about the women."[5]

There is also a level of machismo associated with the act of even covering these issues, at least in my experience. When male journalists and academics research and write about drug trafficking, it's broadly perceived as ballsy, even if those men have children. When I tell people what I do, they often question whether that's a smart or appropriate move for a woman with kids. "Let's face it," Rodgers says, "a lot of the researchers are male in quite a macho way. There's a kind of sexual machismo around saying I study this and that."[6]

As a woman covering drugs and crime in Latin America for nearly fifteen years, I noticed right away the invisibility of women in these spaces and the lack of female narratives that go beyond gender stereotypes. The women who tend to become visible to the mainstream are romantically involved with narcos—women such as Emma Coronel, El Chapo's wife. But it's not because women haven't been involved in these sorts of criminal enterprises, at all levels, from the very beginning.

THE MALE GAZE?

The point here is not to criticize the formidable body of work that exists around organized crime but to highlight that we all have lenses through which we see the world. I am making my best efforts to be very clear about mine: My work is motivated by and a product of my position as a woman in the world. When I'm researching, I want to speak to the women in the room, and when I speak to the men, it's about their relationships with and views of those women. I don't think this has been common practice in the past, but as Elaine Carey's work shows, neither am I the first to do this.

Dr. Felia Allum, in her extensive research on women in the Italian mafia, attacks what she calls the "male gaze" in coverage of organized crime. Allum, a senior lecturer at the University of Bath in the UK, told me, "We only see half of the picture, half of the photo, because it is mainly men who are looking. They are using a male filter, a male lens only, and so [they] only see men as they look at their own reflections." She added that the work of women researching organized crime can often reflect the same male-centered understanding of gender and power. Essentially, it's an approach that characterizes women as sexual objects and victims, and fails to view them from angles and perspectives that contradict or vary from those roles. It doesn't consider women's agency or their influence on the men around them, often because powerful women in organized crime don't fit the tropes created by male protagonists in the business. Not all power brokers walk the walk and talk the talk like Pablo Escobar or El Chapo.[7]

The victimization of and violence against women is a major characteristic of the drug trade and crime in general, but while women in the drug trade are hugely vulnerable to this violence, that is not all they are. The role of wives and girlfriends is also key in the drug trade, but I believe it is underestimated and misunderstood. The importance of women in organized crime who are connected to powerful men via blood, marriage, or romance tends to be minimized. On the flipside, the overwhelming majority of men in organized crime tend to get into the business due to their family or marital ties as well, but this fact is not used as a means of marginalizing their power.

Allum argues that looking at women solely as victims doesn't allow us to clearly see the possible range of roles they might play. It robs women of their agency, Allum says.[8] Her work suggests that women in the Italian mafia function rather like a reserve army and step in when their husbands or male family members are incarcerated.[9]

Considering the full picture, or at least one closer to reality regarding women's roles in organized crime, forces us to face an uncomfortable truth. As a society, we often resist certain perspectives because they bring into question the fundamental understanding on which we subconsciously rely. Our beliefs that women's roles are usually those of the nurturing mother, the good wife, make us feel safe.

Women are often not considered directly responsible for crimes because of their gender—we are encouraged from birth in patriarchal cultures to perceive only men as capable of criminal intent.[10]

We prefer to tell ourselves that women are coerced and co-opted into committing crimes. The existence of bad, evil, deviant women who have the audacity to step out of the accepted gender roles of mothers, caretakers, homemakers, and nurturers to (also) smuggle and sell drugs threatens the very basis on which many civilizations are built. This dynamic helps men to be much more visible in the criminal sphere, creating a hypermasculine culture that can seem to exclude women. But experts also told me that women in the criminal underworld use the fact that they're constantly underestimated to their advantage. "It was because they were underestimated that they managed to rise to the top so quickly," said one female US prosecutor about cases involving high-powered women in the drug trade.[11]

In the case of Digna Valle, her power within the organization was a well-kept secret. Who would have suspected that the Valle brothers' elder sister was also so heavily involved in drug trafficking? She was so sure that she had stayed under the radar that she flew to a meeting in Miami, never suspecting that the DEA had already indicted her and that she would be arrested there. Similarly, Marllory Chacón Rossell, who you will read about in chapter 3, was a glamorous middle-class woman who traveled around the world as part of her money laundering and drug trafficking activities for years before she caught the attention of the DEA. She counted some of the highest-ranking members of the Guatemalan government among her allies and still faces no drug trafficking charges at home.

"Smart women employ the gendered tropes to their advantage. This has helped when being prosecuted. They are the 'victim,'" said Carey.[12] A lawyer who has represented a number of powerful female drug traffickers in the US justice system described witnessing an older female client on the stand in the courtroom play up the role of the clueless grandmother who had been taken advantage of.[13] Women are used by gangs in Central America to deliver extortion messages and collect payments from victims, largely because they are less likely to be stopped and arrested by police.

Women are multidimensional beings—not just victims or mothers, not just vulnerable or submissive. But simplistic stories that revolve around stereotypical heroes and villains, victims and perpetrators are seductive. They form the backbone of countless narratives in the media and in daily life. But in my experience, those binaries do not reflect human nature.

It is not only our view of women that is limited when we see organized crime represented in the media and in popular culture. Men in organized crime are also often portrayed as one-dimensional. They tend to be bombastic, violent, and hypermasculine, a stereotype that leaves little space for the diversity of real-life experiences. Gay men have so far been almost invisible as central figures in organized crime, something that has been challenged with the appearance of fictional characters such as Pacho Herrera, a gay Colombian trafficker in the Netflix series *Narcos*, and Omar Little, the gay Black Baltimore gangster with a heart in the HBO series *The Wire*. But generally, men visible in organized crime in the media, academia, and fiction are reduced to tropes that are centered around narratives that sell and captivate rather than reflect reality.

El Chapo is perhaps the ultimate contemporary example of a male drug trafficking legend. His capture and subsequent trial and life sentence in a court in New York in 2019 was one of the biggest drug trafficking trials of our generation, and it generated millions of words in the press and hours of TV coverage. Bonnie Klapper, a former federal narcotics prosecutor in the US turned criminal lawyer, has defended several high-profile women on drug charges. She told me, "If the female Chapo is out there, she's not being charged, because people aren't looking for her."[14]

VIOLENCE IS NOT THE ONLY PRISM

Klapper raises a pertinent point. Our understanding of women in the trade is based on a pattern set by the legendary men we already know. Women who are violent and who build networks in ways that can be compared to Chapo or Escobar—which includes some of the protagonists in this book. Sebastiana Cottón Vásquez and Marixa Lemus Pérez, as well as historic figures such as Colombian "homicidal godmother" Griselda Blanco Restrepo, are the most visible. When I read about Blanco, and then discovered Cottón and Lemus, I fell into that way of thinking too: Amazing! They're violent and powerful! Women's empowerment? Tick.

But I think that was a mistake. Women who are powerful in a violent sense are in some ways the exception to the rule of women in drug trafficking. We tend to notice their violence to the exclusion of everything else, because that is the prism through which we perceive power in organized crime, a product of the male gaze. That's not just a reflection of gender stereotypes but more literally the way that men (and some women) document organized crime through a lens that puts violence, and only violence, at the center of power. Much like the Chapos and Escobars of this world, women who do wield violent power rarely kill their rivals with their own hands: they have employees to do that for them. The violence they mete out is often delegated, and so it is less direct.

American journalist turned security analyst Douglas Farah experienced that firsthand. After Colombian drug boss Pablo Escobar was finally tracked down and killed in December 1993, Farah went to his funeral, which took place on a rainy day in Medellín. "It was probably a mistake," Farah told me, laughing, years later in an interview. "It was almost a fatal mistake." He chuckles about it now, but he wasn't laughing at the time.[15]

Hermilda de los Dolores Gaviria Berrío, Escobar's mother, was at the funeral.[16] She was a tremendously influential person in the Medellín Cartel, said Farah, but she was almost never mentioned. "I went [to the funeral] with the guy from the *Los Angeles Times*. I can sort of blend in. But this guy was like six foot three tall, bien [really] gringo. And she sees us and starts pointing at us, saying, '*Esos hijos de puta mataron a mi hijo!* [These sons of bitches killed my son!],' pointing at us, as the foreign press. And so [the men who were with her] started kicking us and spitting on us. It was raining, and we were on this little grassy knoll, and as we were trying to get away, we kept slipping on our asses. It was like a really bad comedy.

"And [Hermilda] was, I mean, she was a piece of work"

The machismo within the drug culture tends to encourage male powerhouses to downplay or hide the women and their power in their organizations. "But we [journalists, researchers] also didn't look very far" either, Farah acknowledges. "We didn't push into understanding family dynamics, and all of these groups. They were all clan structures."

"There's an illusion between power and violence. So women who use violence are assumed to be demonstrating their empowerment," says Mo Hume, a professor at the University of Glasgow, Scotland, who has studied women, crime, and violence extensively. By that logic, Hume points out, those who aren't violent aren't powerful.

"Power doesn't work like that. Power circulates. It's a kind of web, it's a network, it's fluid, and it's not static. So I think we need to rethink some of our questions around that. And I think that also applies to men. When we look at men and when men appear, you know, it's the gangster, hypermasculine, whatever, which is also very reductive in terms of their masculinity in their identities."[17]

A BRIEF HISTORY

When Elaine Carey gave her presentation in Salt Lake City, she introduced her audience to a pioneer. A brown woman in the early twentieth century in post-Revolution Mexico, María Dolores Estévez Zuleta is the earliest known example of how, since the dawn of the illicit drugs business and the "drug war" we still see roiling today, women in the region have been at the helm making, smuggling, moving, and selling narcotics.[18]

At the time of her rise to power, Estévez embodied more than an incredible story: She was an existential threat to the powers that be. Her involvement in the drug trade violated the gender stereotypes and expectations of the time, and—perhaps as diabolically—brought her the kind of wealth and status that far exceeded that of others of her race and class, Carey explains in her book.[19]

1920s–1980s

Photos of "Public Enemy Number 1"—part of a decree issued by Mexican president Manuel Ávila Camacho in 1945—show a small woman with long dark hair and deep brown skin. Born in 1906 and brought up in the brassy neighborhood of La Merced in Mexico City, María Dolores Estévez Zuleta might never have imagined when she started running marijuana and morphine for her mother at the age of just thirteen that she would live to found and grow a drug empire that reached over the US/Mexico border and into the United States. At the time, a woman of her complexion and class in Mexican society would have faced discrimination, colorism, and overall disdain from those around her. To have built such a successful organization was no small feat. She became known as Lola "La Chata" and was one of the first major transnational drug traffickers in Mexico, according to archival material put together by Carey and other historians and scholars. She was certainly the first female narco boss in Mexican history.[20]

When the US government learned that Mexico was planning to arrest a prominent narco trafficker, Federal Bureau of Narcotics (FBN) director Harry J. Anslinger was likely surprised at what he read in the information file that was sent along with word of the impending detention: the wanted criminal was female. Up until then, women in the drug business were understood as either narcotics users or pushers.[21]

By the early twentieth century, Mexico was already a transit point for opium headed to the US. Years before, newly arrived Chinese immigrants had begun growing poppies and manufacturing opium in the country's northern states of Sonora and Sinaloa. The US government passed the Harrison Narcotics Act at the end of 1914, which effectively criminalized opium production, leading to a subsequent illicit trade boom as addiction and demand surged.[22]

When girls like Estévez—poor, brown, with little access to education—grew up to be women, they had little access to the post–Mexican Revolution opportunities that women of higher classes embraced. For her, life was about the hustle, which she learned in La Merced, and from her mother. As demand for opium and marijuana spiked, opportunity knocked. Estévez's mother went from peddling fried pork rind *chicharrones* and coffee to selling opium and weed. Estévez followed her example and expanded from selling drugs out of her own tiny market stall to trafficking from her home and eventually moving her product across the border into the US, where demand and profits were greater. She married a former Mexican police officer, Enrique Jaramillo, and they used his contacts from the force to help oil their business. Lola's own ability, however, was what made her unique compared to other women in the trade," Carey writes. "Her relationship with Jaramillo contributed to her business, but both Mexican and US authorities regarded her as an equal, if not superior, trafficker and dealer compared to her husband."[23]

Lola's mother was as crucial as her husband in determining her criminal future. Existing narratives of women in the drug trade tend to focus on how men influence their wives, sisters, daughters, and lovers to get into the narco business. Generally, the wives and girlfriends of major narcos are the women who are visible in media coverage and representations in popular culture. But what has been largely ignored is how women influence each other in this sphere, through relationships between mothers and daughters, sisters, female friends, and business associates.

These interlocking and overlapping relationships between women and women, as well as men and men, are an ever-changing and evolving dynamic in criminal clans, as they are in any group or family. Who is related to whom, who is sleeping with whom, who is friends with whom—these are the dynamics of life. Yet when we are trying to understand influence within gangs and cartels, the emphasis tends to lie on men's control over women and not much else. Women also have control over men and other women, which we need to take into consideration.

Both Estévez and her mother got their businesses started in the local market, a space in which women dominated and moved freely. The same can be said for family homes, where another trafficker—Ignacia Jasso, who became known as "La Nacha"—also began her drug trafficking activities and overlapped with Lola la Chata in the early twentieth century.[24]

Estévez's mother was key to her becoming Lola la Chata, and Lola would also bring her two daughters, Dolores and Maria Luisa, into the business. La Nacha also got her girls involved. In my research for this book, I saw a pronounced pattern of women bringing other females into the trade. From Lola la Chata to Maria, a weapons trafficker whom I met in Mexico City's Tepito neighborhood, to our matriarch Digna Valle, who brought her children, including her daughter Tesla, into the business, women have been fundamental in influencing other females and determining their criminal fate. This matriarchal dynamic in narratives relating the history of the drug trade has been largely missed or minimized.

La Nacha was married to a prominent trafficker. When he was killed, she started using the contacts he had established to source and sell dope out of her home, taking over running his drug production operation. She, like Lola, brought her family into the trade and eventually grew to be such a threat—because of the amount of dope she was providing to consumers across the border—that the US wanted to extradite her. It never happened. Instead, La Nacha was arrested and incarcerated in Mexico, and during that time her daughters continued running her business operations.[25] La Nacha died a free woman sometime in the 1980s. Both she and Lola outlived many of their male contemporaries in the field.

1970s to the present day

Around the time that La Nacha died, female protagonists in the drug trade were making headlines and becoming more visible to the DEA, which was created in the early 1970s. "Women have a prominent place in Latin America's illicit drug traffic, filling every role from 'mule' (courier) to head of a criminal organization," says a 1975 article in the *New York Times*, following the arrest of a number of prominent female traffickers in Mexico, Colombia, and Argentina.[26] Along with the opium and marijuana that La Nacha and Lola la Chata had been shifting was a new addition, cocaine, which was surging north from its production base in the mountains of South America. At that time, women were bossing some of the routes between South America and major US cities.

One of the women who was drawing the attention of law enforcement in the mid-1970s, according to the *New York Times*, was Yolanda Sarmiento, who is described as a "short, stocky, middle aged woman of Chilean descent who owns three wig shops in Buenos Aires." Rhyn C. Tryal, head of the DEA in Argentina at the time, described her as "one of the sharpest dealers anywhere,"[27] and agency declarations said she was "among the most sought-after criminal narcotics organizers in the world."[28]

Sarmiento lived in Argentina from the age of twenty, where she ran a hipster wig and hat shop that she used as a legitimate front for her drug trafficking business that focused on moving cocaine from South America, as well as European heroin, into the US. An innovator, she jumped on the fact that South America's wine industry—like its cocaine trade—was booming and used wine bottles to disguise small packets of drugs for transportation to the US. She was as violent as she was smart, and she was eventually indicted for—among other things—murdering a drug dealing rival in New York and hacking the body to pieces in a bathtub herself, because her husband couldn't face the task.[29] She also helped her man break out of prison.

Her contemporary, Griselda Blanco, is perhaps one of the most infamous patronas of all time. A key cocaine supplier to New York from her base in Medellín, Colombia, she worked her way up from the bottom, using violence and her social networks to create a formidable transnational drug trafficking operation. Blanco named her son Michael Corleone after the character played by Al Pacino in the *Godfather* movies, clearly romanced by the world in which she moved. But her power didn't just come from violence. She was a fast learner, and adaptable. After marrying a smuggler, she started off in the human smuggling business and learned how to forge documents. She then moved into the cocaine trade, which boomed, and is also rumored to have mentored Pablo Escobar.

Blanco's husbands and lovers were fundamental in her early criminal career—something that we see throughout the lives of women in organized crime. Being connected to powerful men in the world of organized crime is often beneficial. Women in Central American gangs very often seek to date members of the Mara Salvatrucha gang (also known as MS-13) as a means of survival. Being attached to these gang members can help give them the security of knowing that other men won't mess with them. It also earns them a (precarious) respect in the community. All women in the drug trade live in the real world and interact with men and other women on a daily basis—sex and connection are inevitable products of daily life.

But there's a double standard at play in the drug trade that plays out in the real world all the time. Women who mix business with sex are accused of "sleeping their way to the top" or using their "feminine wiles" to get what they want. Their sexual relationships are often placed front of stage to explain their rise or their power or their influence, which marginalizes them. Their sexual behavior is often all we see, and that reductionism is loaded with moral judgments implying that women use sex to advance their interests or chances of survival. Meanwhile, men do exactly the same thing but simply aren't judged for it.

During El Chapo's trial in New York, a key witness against him was a woman named Andrea Vélez, his former personal assistant. She is one of the few witnesses who had the nerve to give a victim impact statement detailing the emotional and psychological effect of his crimes on her. For a time, she was also his mistress, and when their relationship soured, he tried to have her killed by a group of Hell's Angels. The assassination plot was unsuccessful. Vélez's testimony revealed that her role in both El Chapo's personal life and his criminal activities was fundamental. It also revealed that she eventually turned FBI informant against him but that she's not holding a grudge. "I forgive you as I hope you can forgive me," she reportedly said to El Chapo in court.[30]

Griselda Blanco, in her effort to work her way up from the bottom, recruited more highly educated women to work with her (one of them, Yaneth Vergara Hernández, is chronicled in chapter 3). Writer Elaine Carey also observes that Blanco had several female friends whom she took on shopping trips, to parties, and to beauty salon sessions, hoping to enlist them to manipulate the men around her and gain an edge. "Her vanity in a sense masked her uncanny ability to read the strengths and weaknesses of the men she associated with," Carey writes, "whether competitors or colleagues."[31] Many of Blanco's female associates would come to testify against her in her eventual trial.

Like Sarmiento and Blanco, other "Queenpins" who have been the focus of popular culture also tend to be presented in the context of their relationships with the men around them. Sandra Ávila Beltrán, for example, and Enedina Arellano Félix are both Mexican cartel women who have been featured in books and TV series. Both were represented in the recent *Narcos: Mexico* series on Netflix, and Ávila Beltrán recently resurfaced with her own channel on TikTok.[32]

You'll be hard-pressed to find an account of Ávila Beltrán that doesn't mention her boyfriends, her good looks, her sex appeal, and her Botox sessions, as well as the drug trafficking family she was born into. She is allegedly the niece of Miguel Ángel Félix Gallardo, widely perceived as the godfather of the Mexican drug trade and the head of what is thought to be Mexico's first drug trafficking syndicate, the Guadalajara Cartel.[33] We know little about her relationship with the women in that drug trafficking dynasty and the influence they had on her power and rise. A 2008 US Congressional Research Service report described her as "a senior member of the Sinaloa Cartel who was instrumental" in building ties with Colombian traffickers.[34] She spent a total of seven years in prison, two of those in isolation, and yet accounts of her reduce her to a stereotypical sex object.

Enedina Arellano Félix, who took over running the Tijuana Cartel in around 2003, after the arrest and extradition of her brothers, is often referred to as a "Narco Mom" ("Narcomami"), going to the heart of one of the most sacred female tropes: women as mothers. Little is public about Arellano Félix—she is known to have studied accounting in a private university, which probably set her up for managing the cartel's finances. Reports portray her as less belligerent and violent than her brothers, although that could be based on assumptions about women's behavior in the drug trade rather than any empirical evidence.[35]

The Narco Mom moniker emphasizes the fact that Arellano Félix has children, juxtaposing the dual roles of mother and drug trafficker. The mother factor in the drug trade is perhaps the most uncomfortable truth of all, because it violates one of our most basic beliefs: that mothers are supposed to be caretakers, home keepers, both kind and nurturing. If women aren't just staying at home to bear children, look after them, and keep their men happy sexually, then they're deviating from several fundamental cultural expectations. These expectations make it taboo to characterize women as ambitious, wily, violent drug traffickers, even when the evidence suggests they actually are. Perhaps it's because of that taboo that the relationships women traffickers have had with their own mothers and other women in their lives have been neglected in the media and in cultural narratives in favor of a focus on how their fathers, husbands, uncles, or brothers have influenced them.[36]

I have never seen a prominent male narco with children referred to as a "Narco Papi."

Whether narco women are mothers, sisters, aunts, wives, lovers, or grandmothers, they certainly aren't just sitting there "stirring the sauce," as Carey puts it. Women have been working in central roles in the dope business for as long as it has existed. And some of them, such as one of the women in our next chapter, have had criminal careers that spanned several decades and multiple criminal organizations.

CHAPTER 3

BETRAYAL WITHIN A FEMALE TRAFFICKING THREESOME

On June 10, 2013, three women met in Guatemala to discuss their transnational cocaine deal. One of those women was a Colombian named Yaneth Vergara Hernández. She was planning to source and package up nearly half a ton of cocaine from her base city of Medellín and move it north through Central America and Mexico to the United States. The other women, Sebastiana Cottón Vásquez and Marllory (pronounced Marjory) Chacón Rossell, were going to help her.

The three women had been in the drug business for decades. All had worked with major male trafficking powerhouses, but many of those narcos had recently been captured and/or extradited. The only man at the meeting that day—Oliverio Fernando Paleaz Solano—was going to coordinate the air route for the drug load. Marllory had organized the gathering at her house to introduce Sebastiana and Yaneth—both of whom she had previously worked with—to each other.

The meeting would set in motion a female-led drug trafficking deal that would be the three women's last. What's more, one of the women there that day was working as a DEA informant and would give up her criminal cohorts in the hope of reducing her own sentence.

Sebastiana was a peasant turned violent plaza boss. She hadn't gone looking for the drug business: it had found her. Illegal shipments of cocaine, marijuana, and heroin had been moving through the rural town of Malacatán, San Marcos, from the day she was born there. The San Marcos border in Guatemala lies up against the state of Chiapas, Mexico, and is a major transit point for cocaine and other drugs arriving from the south and moving north into Mexico. This daily traffic of goods takes place under the watchful eye of regional crime syndicates such as the Sinaloa Cartel, which was one of Sebastiana's clients. Just like Digna Valle in Honduras, Sebastiana was responsible for making sure the cartel's shipments made it safely across the border.

Marllory was another story. A middle-class girl with a university education, she was worldly, sophisticated, and smart, with some legitimate business experience. Married to a money launderer, she had stepped in to take over the business after he ended up in jail for handling the ill-gotten gains of Colombian organized crime. When I picture them meeting in Marllory's house that day, Marllory is well-dressed, with immaculate hair and makeup. Sebastiana is shorter, rounder, and rougher around the edges, with a malevolent smirk that shines through in the pictures of her from court documents and media stories.

But where Yaneth sits in the room, there is only a black silhouette.

———————

The letter was handwritten, sent from the Aliceville federal prison in Alabama. Addressed to me, it had been sent to *VICE* headquarters in New York, in response to a slew of letters I had sent to all of the women that I investigated for this book. Yaneth, now in her early sixties, was the only woman to respond.

When *VICE* reception emailed me in mid-October 2021 with a photo of her letter, I noticed the return address on the envelope, and my heart skipped a beat. Of all the women I had been researching, Yaneth was the most invisible and mysterious. There were no available photos that I could find, no mugshots. She was an enigma, an unseen person. So she was the last person I had expected to hear from.

"I hope you're in the best health," she wrote. "Apologies for not answering your letter sooner, everything has been so difficult because of COVID. . . . I want you to explain to me what you need. I was detained in the '80s and got out in the '90s, as you know I worked for some time with Griselda Blanco and others."[1]

That was news to me. Griselda Blanco is the region's most famous female drug trafficker. Bar none. During the 1980s, Griselda was a major player in the cocaine business, and during that time she surrounded herself with men and women—many of the latter much more educated and well-heeled than she was—to create a transnational drug trafficking network that made her the stuff of legend. Yaneth had apparently been one of those women, and I realized then that her current stint in prison was her second time around for trafficking. Later, I discovered that she had been in the drug trade since the 1970s, when she was in her twenties. She was first arrested in the early '80s and served seven years in the US. When she was released in 1990 and deported back to Colombia, she said she tried to go straight for a while but struggled to make enough money to support her son. She went back to cocaine trafficking in 1997, she told me, "because of need."

Hers is the longest criminal career of all of the women I investigated. And here she was writing to me. I was stunned and delighted.

"The other two people are out now," she wrote when I asked about the setup in 2013, "and the one I stay in touch with is Sebastiana [Cottón Vásquez]."[2]

But Yaneth had known Marllory longer, and it was to her that she reached out for help when one of her earlier drug deals ran out of road.

THE FALL OF HER KINGPIN

"Fair to say it's difficult to be a woman in a male-dominated world?" Michael Nadler, a US prosecutor, asked Yaneth in a Miami courtroom in late February 2018. She was testifying during the trial of Jesús

López Londoño, alias "Mi Sangre" ("My Blood" in English), who, during his reign was one of the most powerful drug traffickers of his generation and an important contact of Yaneth's.

"Yes," she answered.

"You had to work extra hard to get these people to like you and know you?" Nadler asked.

"Yes," she said.[3]

López was one of the leaders of Los Urabeños drug trafficking organization in Colombia when Yaneth was in the business. The group was born out of the violent paramilitaries that went up against the country's guerrilla armies in the civil conflict that lasted for more than fifty years. Both the guerrillas and the paramilitaries financed their activities, at least in part, through the international cocaine trade.

Back then, López's group was moving cocaine out of Colombia and up the coasts to Central America and Mexico in go-fast boats. Los Urabeños charged other traffickers and brokers a tax to move their drugs through certain parts of the country. That was the motive for his and Yaneth's meeting in 2010: she had to pay a toll to move her cocaine loads from Medellín north to the coastal cities of Necolí and Turbo.

Her motive for appearing in court that day was to help the US government bury López in the hope of a lighter sentence for herself. Yaneth had been sentenced in 2016 to eighteen years behind bars. She had been brought to the courtroom from her Alabama jail cell to testify against López. This is a constant dynamic between the protagonists in organized crime in the US judicial system— less powerful traffickers testifying against the higher-ups that they worked with.

"[H]e was in the high command of the organization," said Yaneth that day in court, and she agreed to pay López to allow her cocaine shipment to pass.

López's trial was a big deal for the US government. At the time, his organization, Los Urabeños, was "the largest and most influential 'BACRIM' ('banda criminal' or criminal group) currently operating in Colombia," according to the Treasury Department, and one of the main sources of the illegal cocaine gushing into the US.[4] López had eluded capture for years until he was finally arrested in Argentina in 2012 and extradited to the United States. He was a big fish, and the Americans were determined to make an example of him. Yaneth was an instrumental witness in a trial via which López was eventually convicted and sentenced to thirty-one years.[5]

Compared to López, Yaneth was unknown. Perhaps that's why she was always preparing for his downfall by developing different relationships as alternative routes for moving her cocaine north. One of those relationships was with Marllory.

THE RISE OF THE QUEENS

Yaneth first reached out to Marllory for help almost a decade before their meeting with Sebastiana in 2013. Back then, Yaneth had an eight-million-dollar problem: a ton of cocaine sitting in Honduras without a buyer. Her original deal had fallen through, and Yaneth contacted Marllory to help her find a new investor, fast. Which is why, on a night in April 2004, Marllory and her husband were sitting at dinner on a ranch in Izabal, Guatemala, a crucial corridor for cocaine traveling northward from Honduras to Mexico and the US.

Marllory's hosts were Eliu Lorenzana-Cordon and his wife, Tavi. Eliu's older brother, Waldemar Lorenzana-Cordon, was also there. The Lorenzana family was one of the "most violent and sophisticated" transnational criminal organizations operating in the world at that time, according to the US Department of Justice.[6] Marllory hoped that Eliu would help her and her amiga by fronting the money for the dope and getting it moving. "We spoke about the logistics for collecting the cocaine [in Honduras] and delivering the dollars, and the price of the cocaine," Marllory recalled years later in court, when she testified against the Lorenzana brothers.[7]

Eliu sized her up as she spoke. His plump face and receding hairline belied his position as one of the country's most powerful drug bosses. He was not used to doing business with women. In her early thirties, with long, light-brown hair and a fair complexion, she was a world away from the faces Eliu usually negotiated with. Decidedly middle-class, Marllory had some university education (she dropped out) and had run a number of small legitimate businesses before entering the drug trafficking world. Her past experiences would help her set up a trail of businesses in the region that she subsequently used to launder her clients' money.

"I don't know you," Eliu said to her, "but by looking in your eyes, I can tell that I can trust you." The deal was on, and so began a relationship that would last for years.[8]

ZACAPA

I was very close to the house where Marllory had her first meeting with the Lorenzana brothers when I visited the city of Zacapa, an hour's drive into Guatemala from its border with Honduras, in March 2021. Two days before, I had been in El Espíritu, talking to Juanita and the other residents of the tiny town, and then to Digna Valle herself, and my nerves were still on edge. I felt as though Digna and the Valle clan were still with me, and now I was driving into Marllory's old stomping ground.

Before Digna's Valle Cartel was taken down by the United States government in 2014, the cocaine they moved across the border would come up through Zacapa, which at the time was controlled by the Lorenzana family. When I passed through, the Lorenzana brothers, Marllory, and the Valles were long gone, but the city of Zacapa and the department in which it is located remain a key trafficking hub. Other narcos have moved in to fill the vacuum the Lorenzanas left.

We had crossed the Honduras-Guatemala border at El Florido, where I had jumped out of my Honduran driver's car to clamber into the Tsuru sedan driven by my Guatemalan driver. My local journalist colleague Julie López sat in the front seat. We drove away from the border into Guatemala, hot, dry air blowing in on us from the road.

Finally, we entered Zacapa, where we were interrupted by a constant beeping from behind. I turned around to look out the back window and saw a heavy black truck behind us. Its driver was honking the horn aggressively to get other cars out of the way so that it could pull off to the right.

There were two men sitting in the back of the truck. Both of them were holding long black automatic weapons and wearing bulletproof vests. They looked agitated and restless. Neither of them wore a police uniform, and the truck was not a police truck. The cars around them were scrambling to get out of their way.

My local contact, let's call him Juan, said quietly, "That's them. They're the law around here."

Juan is a former employee of the Lorenzanas, and when we met, he'd already lived one life despite being just in his thirties. He started working for the family when he was just twelve years old, he told me, as we sat together at a table in a local restaurant. One of his jobs had been bringing weapons in from Honduras. Then he started doing drugs and hanging out with the cartel's heavies, who were the armed wing of the Lorenzana's organization.

"Most of my youth I lost totally involved in that world," he said.

The night in 2004 when Marllory first met with Eliu and Waldemar in Guatemala, she was already an accomplished money launderer. The dinner with the Lorenzana brothers marked the start of a fruitful relationship that would earn her the title of "one of the most prolific narcotics traffickers in Central America," from the US Treasury Department.[9]

"Marllory was a very smart and bright person with some very high-level entrepreneurial skills," Steve Fraga told me. Fraga was a DEA agent for thirty years and spent a lot of his time investigating drug trafficking in Central America. "I think she was a person who saw some opportunities and took successful advantage of them. She had a business-oriented mindset." Had Marllory applied herself to a Fortune 500 company rather than the drug trade, Fraga said, things would have turned out very differently for her. "Just like in legitimate business," he said, "where there are women all over the world who are CEOs, in the same way there are women all over the world who are CEOs or heads of drug trafficking organizations or play very prominent roles in those organizations."[10]

My guide in Zacapa, Juan, remembered seeing Marllory about town when they were both working for the Lorenzana clan. "She was a woman with a big presence and very intimidating because of the kind of people she was surrounded by, and the amount. Because she moved with security everywhere. There was always someone at the door."[11] By the time Juan reached his late teens, he was burned out and left the mafia. But Marllory stayed, rising higher and higher in the ranks.

"The power that [the Lorenzanas] had with people was incredible," Juan said. "They controlled everything. And they had their own private army. And they had the police looking after them. Marllory was guarded by the National Police."[12] The National Police escort signaled her growing relationships with the government in Guatemala. Her friends in high places were also increasingly under scrutiny, including the country's then vice president, Roxana Baldetti, and the interior minister, Mauricio López Bonilla. At that time, López Bonilla—who provided Marllory with her National Police escort—was the highest-ranking security official working with the Americans on the bilateral anti-narcotics fight. Some reporting claims that she had met with Baldetti[13] and invited López Bonilla to her home for a meeting in 2013, by which point she had been sanctioned by the US Treasury for drug trafficking and money laundering.[14]

Baldetti has always vehemently denied knowing Marllory, but López Bonilla never has. It remains unclear why he provided a police escort for her if he was aware she was under investigation by the United States for her involvement in the drug trade.

When Marllory was sanctioned in 2012, the US government said she was laundering $10 million in drug profits every month. When the sanctions were issued, the director of the US Department of the Treasury's Office of Foreign Assets Control, Adam J. Szubin, said,

"Marllory Chacon's drug trafficking activities and her ties to the Mexican drug cartels make her a critical figure in the narcotics trade."[15]

The move by the US government pressured Marllory to consider her future, and that of her business associates.

LA REFORMA

Less than an hour's drive from Zacapa lies the tiny town of La Reforma, which was once home to the Lorenzana brothers. It is just off Highway CA9, which runs from the eastern coast of Honduras all the way to Guatemala City and onward to the western coast—a route known locally and in bilateral law enforcement efforts as the "cocaine highway." When I asked Juan if it was safe to drive from Zacapa to La Reforma, he sucked in his breath and shook his head slowly. But then he pointed out to me and my driver on Google Maps where in La Reforma the mansions of the former drug bosses were located, so we could at least drive by for a look.

Before Eliu and Waldemar Lorenzana were arrested in 2011 and 2013, respectively, they—like their drug trafficking father before them—were loved and feared in these parts. When DEA agents and Guatemalan officers first tried to detain them in 2009, the locals rose up in their defense, according to media reports at the time. Video shows hundreds of people gathered in the streets holding placards that say, "Lorenzana Family we're with you," and "DEA—*injusticia para la humanidad* [The DEA is inhumane]."[16]

When we drove from Zacapa to La Reforma that day in March 2021, I did feel apprehensive as I watched the dry yellowed fields speed by. In towns like these, outsiders are instantly noticed.

Initially, La Reforma felt like any other small pueblo. But as we drove through, I noticed a number of very large houses that dwarfed the other residences, most of which were one-story cement-block structures. New trucks and cars lined the streets in a town in which the average resident probably couldn't afford to buy a secondhand sedan. The local fire station looked too well-equipped for such a small settlement. Juan said that the Lorenzanas frequently stepped in to supply the kind of services that the state should have been financing.

A CLOSE CALL FOR AN OUTSIDER

When Sebastiana Cottón Vásquez visited La Reforma, she didn't receive a very warm welcome. In fact, she found herself outnumbered and outgunned. It was 2008, and she was pissed. She'd paid $3 million to Waldemar (whom she called Don Walde) for some four hundred kilos of cocaine, but the dope had never turned up, and she was convinced he had stolen it from her. When she called to bawl him out, they got into a shouting match during which he told her to come down to his ranch if she wanted to discuss it further. Sebastiana lived in Malacatán, on Guatemala's western coast, close to her country's border with Mexico. From there, she facilitated and controlled the transportation of drugs into Mexico for clients including the Lorenzanas and the Sinaloa Cartel.

The trip to Waldemar's ranch was a substantial one for her. But she went anyway, because there was $3 million at stake, and she wanted answers.

As soon as she walked onto the veranda of Waldemar's house, Sebastiana—who described the incident during her testimony years later in a Washington, DC, courtroom—knew she had made a mistake. More than a hundred armed men emerged from the garden, surrounding the veranda where she and her small group stood with Waldemar and his colleague, another Guatemalan trafficker, Don Juancho. A helicopter circled overhead.[17]

Sebastiana told the court that she had arrived with just four of her closest allies: her cousin Max, her son Antonio, a Mexican associate named Lucas, and another employee named Rudy. She was the only woman there. Waldemar told them to sit down at a table on the veranda, and as they did, the armed men closed in. He and Don Juancho slammed their guns down on the table, pointed at Sebastiana and Lucas. They shouted and jabbed their fingers in the air, indignant at being accused of stealing. They claimed they had sent the cocaine that Sebastiana had paid for in a truck with hidden compartments.

"Every time I moved," Sebastiana said, "whether it was just shifting to get more comfortable in the chair, Don Juancho would touch his gun."

In an attempt to cool things off, she got up to use the bathroom, but when she came back, her cousin Max took her aside. "Doña Tana," he said, "let's get out of here.[18] Things have gotten ugly. Don Juancho has told me that if you make any moves, any movements, he's going to shoot you."

Meanwhile, Waldemar and Rudy were screaming at each other, and when Sebastiana took her seat again, Lucas started kicking her foot under the table. He looked at her and mouthed, "Vámonos! Vámonos! [Let's go!]" The situation was spiraling out of control.

Sebastiana got to her feet calmly. "The big fish has eaten the little fish, and I will figure [it] out," she said to the men around her. Without having the drugs she had purchased, she now owed her Mexican buyer the $3 million he had fronted for them. "I'll figure out how to pay that money," she told Waldemar.

The men quieted, and the tension dispersed. Her group stood up and walked out, unhurt. According to Sebastiana, neither the cocaine nor the money ever appeared.

The next time Sebastiana saw Waldemar was at the home of his brother Eliu, also in La Reforma. When he caught sight of her, she said he panicked. He seemed certain that she was going to have her revenge over the missing $3 million.

"Look, Doña Tana," he said, according to Sebastiana's testimony, "if you're going to do something to me, do it face to face, because I'm not going to just stand by for it."

Sebastiana said she was nonplussed during this interaction when she recounted the exchange in court. "So I just smiled and asked him, 'Are you crazy or what?'"

But Sebastiana's smile is anything but reassuring. A photo of her during trial shows a woman with a complex smile that is at once menacing, mocking, and confident. It contains a hint of violence. It suggests that she is not to be messed with.

Sebastiana, unlike Marllory, had grown up an impoverished peasant girl in Malacatán, born in what Guatemala's chief anti-narcotics prosecutor Gerson Alegría described as "a key strategic point" in the international drug trade.[19] Sebastiana's hometown is a major land entry point to Mexico as well as a key maritime drug route because of the Pacific Ocean to the west. Her life there was hard. The men around her were hard. She left school after second grade, but she avoided going home. "My father abused my mother in front of me all the time," Sebastiana told Judge Marcia Cooke during one of her sentencing hearings in Miami in 2015. "[He] was an alcoholic and did not support our family."[20]

When she was eighteen, Sebastiana told the court, she was abducted by a man who eventually became her husband and the father of her five children. "[He] was a very angry and violent man and very domineering. I lived in fear while he was around," she said.

When he eventually abandoned her, she began selling contraband to feed her kids. Soon after that, she married again, this time a local drug boss. When he was killed, she took over his business, according to a source from a rival organization who spoke to me on condition of anonymity. We met in a café in downtown Guatemala City in March 2021 to discuss Sebastiana, and the source was nervous. They came wearing a cap and a facemask (it was during the COVID-19 pandemic) but couldn't sit still or stop looking around. They had once had a personal run-in with Sebastiana's family that they asked me not to describe for fear that it would identify them. They called Sebastiana a violent hothead, from personal experience.[21]

But Sebastiana's defense lawyer, William Clay, argued to a US judge that geography, more than marriage or temperament, was the main dynamic that brought her into the trafficking world. "I just want you to understand," he told the court. "Single mother, all of these problems, a sense of insecurity, economic security and physical security, from having been violated in a country that the State Department calls one of the most dangerous countries in Central America. . . . That's the environment she was in, in a rural area, dominated by very machismo, very bad, violent men."[22]

Over the years, Sebastiana developed a deadly reputation in the region. She had connections to Digna Valle's cartel in Honduras and other drug trafficking powerhouses to the south, in Colombia, and to the north, in Mexico. She was a frequent face in Culiacán, where she worked with El Chapo's Sinaloa Cartel. "This is somebody who was known through Guatemala, known through Mexico, as a woman who should be feared because she had the ability to make a lot of things happen," said US prosecutor Monique Botero during Sebastiana's sentencing.

During her trafficking career, Sebastiana was arrested by federal security forces—and subsequently freed for unknown reasons—a number of times in Mexico, according to local media.[23] Much like the cocaine she trafficked, she moved fluidly between San Marcos in Guatemala, and Chiapas, the bordering state in Mexico.

BETRAYAL

By the time Marllory brought Yaneth and Sebastiana together at that meeting in June 2013, many of the men they had worked with were behind bars. The Lorenzana mafia had been dismantled, the brothers sentenced to life in prison.[24] One of Sebastiana's other key local contacts, Juan Alberto Ortiz López, alias Juan Chamale, had been arrested in 2011. And Yaneth's former associate and trafficking lynchpin Jesús López Londoño, "Mi Sangre," who she eventually came to testify against, was also in custody by that point.

So the women did their own deal, the details of which I was able to piece together from court documents. When I was comparing those documents, the penny finally dropped on who it must have been that eventually tipped off the DEA about their plans. According to Sebastiana's plea agreement, a person identified as a "Confidential Source" (CS) met with Yaneth, Sebastiana, and Fernando Paleaz, the air route coordinator, in June 2013, to "negotiate the receipt and transport of a 450-kilogram cocaine shipment from La Guajira, Colombia, to Rio Dulce, Guatemala."[25] Hundreds of Blackberry messages and video and audio recordings were sent to the CS documenting the movement of the shipment. Yaneth sent pictures of the shipment to the informant in October, saying it was ready for departure and that Paleaz should send the plane to pick it up. The source in turn showed those Blackberry messages to DEA agents: "The pictures clearly showed packaged bundles, bricks of cocaine and a brick displaying the marking on the cocaine as 'RANA.'"[26] *Rana* means toad or frog in Spanish, and it was likely the marking the group agreed on to identify the shipment.

Late on the evening of January 10, 2014, the cocaine left the coastal department of La Guajira in a Seneca aircraft en route to Guatemala. La Guajira is located in northeastern Colombia, where it borders Venezuela and sits on the Caribbean Sea. It's a popular departure point for cocaine headed to Caribbean islands or the eastern coast of Central America.

Again, according to Sebastiana's plea agreement, Yaneth messaged the CS to say that the shipment was on its way. On the morning of January 11, the load arrived in Guatemala, where it was seized by the DEA.[27]

The identity of the CS remains confidential in Sebastiana's court documents. But Yaneth's plea agreement states clearly that it was Marllory who received all of the communications from Yaneth about the cocaine shipment.[28] Marllory, faced with sanctions and drug trafficking charges in the US, appears to have decided to betray her female colleagues in exchange for a lighter sentence and was passing information about the deal to the DEA, even as she executed it.

It was most likely an error that the plea agreements for Yaneth and Sebastiana carried different information, but what happened following the seizure of that load also points to Marllory as the informant: She turned herself in to the authorities in Miami in September 2014, just before her criminal cohorts were arrested.[29] Sebastiana was detained in Mexico the following month.[30] In November, Yaneth was arrested in Colombia.[31]

Now in custody herself, Marllory was protected from any possible attempts at revenge by the former female colleagues she had betrayed. Realizing what Marllory had done helped me understand why, in her letters, Yaneth had said she maintained contact only with Sebastiana. After a wide-ranging criminal career, Marllory was looking at the possibility of a life sentence for the charges against her in Miami. It was only logical that she would agree to make a deal. "The Queen of the South," as she was dubbed, had her five children to consider. Her eldest daughter, Stefanel Castellanos Chacón, had also been targeted by the US government for laundering money and overseeing some twenty-four companies, ranging from hotels and construction companies to clothing stores. Before turning herself in to US authorities, Marllory, something of a fashion icon, paid her girl a visit in Paris, a sort of last hurrah. Guatemalan celebrity magazine *Contrapoder* featured pictures of Marllory and Stefanel flaunting their wealth, allegedly in the French capital, some two months before Marllory went to Miami to surrender to the authorities. And less than four years later, in early 2019, Marllory was a free woman again.

I made numerous attempts to interview Marllory for this book. She was in the process of applying for a visa that would give her the right to live and work in the US, and I was told that she didn't want to jeopardize that process by talking to me.

Sebastiana was released some six months after Marllory, in October 2019, and, according to sources in Guatemala, she has gone back to her old haunts on the Guatemala-Mexico border. Whether she has gone back to trafficking I do not know, but the source I interviewed in Guatemala City who knew her personally said, "If she doesn't go back to that, what else is she going to do? She doesn't know anything else."[32]

As for Yaneth, as I was finishing this book, she was awaiting deportation to Colombia after being released from prison in September 2022.

I am waiting to hear how much more she might be willing to tell me.

CHAPTER 4

THE WOMEN OF
THE MARA SALVATRUCHA

Guatemala, where Sebastiana, Yaneth, and Marllory got acquainted, lies in the heart of Central America, which is a base not just for drug cartels but for the notorious Mara Salvatrucha street gangs (also known as MS-13 and the Barrio 18), which have metastasized across the region. But the story of women in the Mara is a different one from that of our other protagonists in the cartels. For the most part, street gangs in Central America remain viscerally misogynist, with a special type of violence reserved for the women who dare betray them.

ISABEL

The groaning and panting of people having sex at such a close proximity to her shocked Isabel. The gasping and cries were distracting as she tried to have sex with her own boyfriend.

"We used to do it on *champas*," Isabel told me when we met in a fast-food chicken restaurant, an hour's drive from central San Salvador, El Salvador. Champas are mattresses covered by sheets to improvise a tent, designed to conceal the two people lying inside, as well as what they are doing. Such measures are necessary during conjugal visits on the patio of the Izalco high security men's prison, when hundreds of women come to visit their gang men. Conjugal visits inevitably meant trying for a discreet fuck, hence the champas, which made the prison patio look like a tiny, improvised refugee camp.

Isabel first met her boyfriend—let's call him Shorty—on Facebook when she was just nineteen years old. "I liked the way he treated me day to day," she said. "He had a lot of attention to detail and is the only man who has ever given me roses."[1]

Looking at Isabel, I found that hard to believe. She met me wearing a short, tight brown jersey dress that only just covered the top of her upper thighs. Her long black hair fell down her back, and her face resembled one out of a Botticelli painting. The decision to start a relationship with a guy who was already serving time in prison for murder blew my mind. Shorty was a member of the Barrio 18 gang, which promised he would spend more time inside than outside prison for the rest of his short, violent life—a fact Isabel understood. Shorty had joined the gang when he was nine years old, she told me, and was wanted for murder by the time he was eleven.

After getting her mother's permission, Isabel went to the Izalco prison, a seventy-kilometer (forty-three-mile) drive from San Salvador, to meet Shorty for the first time after corresponding via Facebook for months. He had gone back to studying on the inside and invited her to his high school graduation ceremony.

"It was the first time I had been in a prison," she remembered. Every week for the next few years, she would visit Shorty and undergo a "full revision" as part of the process of getting into the penitentiary. That meant first stripping naked in a small cubicle. Then she would get up on a chair to squat so that a female prison guard could insert her fingers inside Isabel to make sure she hadn't stashed any drugs or contraband in her vagina or anus. Apparently, this is one of the common methods for sneaking prohibited items into El Salvador's jails.

"You get used to it—it becomes routine," Isabel said. "At first it was humiliating, but afterwards you forget about it. You can get used to anything."

The things you do for love, I thought. I couldn't think of any other reason she would keep going back to the hellholes of Latin America's prisons.

Over the past few decades, the Mara Salvatrucha gangs have spread across the Northern Triangle countries of El Salvador, Honduras, and Guatemala, with as many as seventy thousand MS-13 members scattered across those nations alone. Formed on the streets of Los Angeles, California, in the late 1970s, the gang began life as a social organization that provided a sense of belonging to marginalized immigrant youths—mostly Salvadoran refugees running from a civil war back home. "The MS13 is a complex phenomenon. The gang is not about generating revenue as much as it is about creating a collective identity that is constructed and reinforced by shared, often criminal experiences, especially acts of violence and expressions of social control," write Steven Dudley, Héctor Silva Ávalos, and Juan José Martínez, who have studied the gangs extensively.[2]

Violence is at the center of the gang's culture and modus operandi, which is why it has long been a focus of law enforcement in both the US and Central America. In the mid-1990s and into the 2000s, thousands of foreign-born gang members convicted of crimes in the US were deported home to Central America, where they formed new cells. They arrived in El Salvador in the wake of a brutal civil war. Of the nearly 130,000 convicted criminals deported to Central America between 2001 and 2010, over 90 percent were sent to El Salvador, Guatemala, or Honduras, according to Department of Homeland Security (DHS) figures quoted by Dudley, Silva Ávalos, and Martínez.[3] Today, overcrowded and poorly resourced prisons in El Salvador are tightly packed with gang members, essentially serving as the criminal headquarters of the MS-13 and Barrio 18.

In 2016, following a spike in homicides in El Salvador, the government imposed "extraordinary measures" in its prisons, designed to cow the gangs. At that time, El Salvador was one of the most homicidal countries in the world, with a murder rate of more than eighty-one per one hundred thousand people. Venezuela, another deeply violent nation in the grip of a social, economic, and humanitarian crisis didn't even come close as the second-worst offender, with fifty-nine murders per one hundred thousand.[4]

Gangs, who were responsible for the majority of the murders, functioned as a parallel government with their leaders headquartered in the prisons.[5] From there, leaders continued to control thousands of gang cells operating on the streets around the country and to manage extortion rackets and street-level drug sales. Using mobile phones, they terrorized and extorted those on the outside. In an attempt to limit this practice, the government confined many incarcerated gang members to their cells, shutting down the cell phone signal in areas around prisons. The government also eliminated conjugal visits between gang members and their partners: the champas disappeared. Isabel and Shorty's amorous trysts in Izalco prison came to a sudden end.

The measures were supposed to be temporary, but they remain in place today. Most recently, they were renewed by the increasingly authoritarian government of the so-called hipster president, Nayib Bukele, a social media whiz who is often seen wearing a leather jacket and a backward baseball cap. In 2022, the Bukele government renewed its gang crackdown, rounding up and imprisoning thousands more gang members, an act that only worsened the levels of overcrowding in the country's prison system.

Shorty was never out of prison for more than a couple of months, according to Isabel. He would complete a sentence and then quickly reoffend. They rarely had more than a few months together on the outside before he was back behind bars.

It wasn't just Shorty who had problems with the law. Isabel said she was constantly harassed by the police because they knew that she was Shorty's girlfriend. "I couldn't sleep in my house—it felt like the police were going to come for me at any moment." On one occasion, she said a police officer arrested her and her brother and took them to the station. He took her out back, and then he put a gun to her head, she remembered. "I began to cry really hard," she said. "He told me he was going to shoot me and then my brother."

He told her to get down on her knees. "No," she said. "No, I'm not going to do that."

"Was that your pride?" I asked her.

"No," she said. "I was terrified that if I did, he would shoot me in the head."

My local colleague Bryan Avelar, who was also present for the interview, asked her, "What's the good side of all this? What's in it for you?"

"I'm respected because I'm his woman," she answered, "because he is admired and respected in the neighborhood."

But even that advantage was deeply limited. "I know if he dies that will all end," she said. The security that she derived from being Shorty's woman seemed utterly precarious, especially given the generally short lifespan of gang members. Isabel was vague about whether she had anything to do with the gang's criminal enterprises, such as extortion or drug sales, but observers and my own research told me that girlfriends, mothers, and sisters who are connected by blood or relationships to gang members are often involved in their criminal activities.

It is often women who take cell phones into the businesses or properties of victims to oblige them to listen to gang members who are calling to terrorize and threaten them from prison. Perhaps this is because they are less likely to draw attention or suspicion than the young men they're working with. Women also frequently collect the extortion profits from the schemes run by the gangs, or lend their bank accounts so that victims can deposit cash there. They also often smuggle the cash into the prisons to their men. "In recent years, women have been known more as gang collaborators—useful to carry out certain criminal tasks for the group (transporting weapons, collecting extortion fees, etc.) as well as domestic responsibilities," said Sonja Wolf, an assistant professor with the drug policy program at the

Centro de Investigación y Docencia Económicas (CIDE) university in Mexico.[6] When I was reporting in Guatemala a few years back, I found that women there were very active in executing extortion schemes,[7] a trend backed up by an Interpeace study on the role of women in Central American gangs.[8]

But women weren't always just the gang's foot soldiers.

BRENDA

The history of street gangs in the US is marked by spikes in atrocious violence. Among the gang-related murders that took place in the late 1990s and early 2000s, one stands out for our purposes: the killing of Brenda Paz in 2003. Originally from Honduras, Brenda was only thirteen when she was "jumped" or initiated into the MS-13 in Dallas. Her actions and subsequent murder would change the history of women in the gang forever, observers told me.

Brenda, who was known in the gang as Smiley, "was different from the other girls," wrote reporter Jamie Stockwell, who covered her murder trial for the *Washington Post*. "She came as close to being a leader as a female could."[9] But that power and standing wasn't enough to protect her.

Her crime, as far as the gang was concerned, was unforgiveable. Brenda was cooperating with law enforcement that was investigating the gang. Research and reporting on her life suggests that Brenda wasn't terribly discreet about her cooperation. She was placed in but eventually left the US Witness Security Program because she felt isolated and lonely. At one point she was helping officers from at least six different states investigate a number of crimes that she had witnessed, including beatings, murder, and theft. She had also committed to testifying for prosecutors in gang murder trials, a fact that could have put the final nail in her coffin.[10]

Despite that, she sought out her former homies, people she thought were still her friends. On July 13, 2003, fellow gang members lured her into a national park in Virginia, where they set upon her. One of her assailants tied a rope around her neck to hold her in place while the others stabbed her sixteen times all over her body.[11] She was four months pregnant at the time. "There's a baby involved. I mean, you have to be sick to actually hold a rope around somebody's neck, hear her screaming and fighting, being tortured and stabbed multiple times in the stomach, legs, and just dying," her friend told CBS News.[12]

Samuel Logan, author of a book about Brenda's murder, spoke about her in an interview with *Immigration Daily*:

> Brenda was the first teenager in the history of the US Witness Protection program to enter without adult supervision. The program, which was designed for middle-aged mob informants, not pregnant teenage girls, failed to provide Brenda with the love and attention she so needed. She was alone too often, and eventually, at the deepest moment of her loneliness, the only person she thought to call was her boyfriend, an MS-13 member. He eventually betrayed her, which is ultimately what led to her death.[13]

Brenda's collaboration with law enforcement established an idea that took strong hold within MS-13 and endures to this day: women are more likely to turn into state witnesses , or "snitches," than men. A couple of years later, her murder contributed to a decision made by the gang leadership during a 2005 meeting in San Salvador. During the meeting, which had been called to discuss the future of MS-13, the role of women came up. Leaders dictated that women were not to be initiated into the gang anymore. They would take on no new female members, and the current female members would be demoted.

As MS-13 cells grew across El Salvador, a nationalist movement took hold within the gang, during which members ceased to name their cliques after streets in the United States, as they had done previously, and started to embrace their local environment more. The banning of women from the gang, according to experts, was a sign that the men in power were also embracing the misogynist cultures of their new home bases.[14]

"Women had been prestigious members of the gang in the US, and that was completely extinguished," says Juan José Martínez, an anthropologist who has studied El Salvador's gangs for years.[15] He and fellow researchers Steven Dudley and Héctor Silva Ávalos write, "In the simplest terms, women are not considered human [by the gang]. They are routinely referred to as 'bichas' or 'hainas,' which, roughly translated, means animals."[16] Another reason for excluding them is that women tend to be the source of romantic and sexual disputes and rivalries within gangs.[17]

Details contained in reporting from court documents for cases against members of MS-13 describe a use of violence against women—disgraced girlfriends and wives and collaborators—that can only be described as medieval.[18] In 2007, local media in El Salvador reported a murder that was as similarly violent and disturbing as Brenda's. The prosecutors described how an MS-13 member known as "El Crimen" (which means "crime") asked for permission to kill a woman who had left her boyfriend, a gang member, when he was in jail. It was an insult to the entire gang, El Crimen reasoned. He was given the green light to kill her.[19]

The woman in question didn't know what was coming until El Crimen took her to a local house and pulled a gun on her. He told her, "Today you're going to show love to all us homeboys, you daughter of a whore." She was raped by at least ten gang members, penetrated in the vagina, the anus, and the mouth, according to the report. El Crimen, still not satisfied that she had suffered enough, then grabbed a small axe and slit her throat, finally decapitating her.[20]

The violence, exclusion, and treatment of women by Central American gangs goes far beyond the supposition that they may turn state's witness. It is cultural. Violence toward women is common and widely accepted. The Northern Triangle countries of El Salvador, Guatemala, and Honduras have some of the worst femicide rates in the world. El Salvador and Honduras are in the global top five nations for deadly hate crimes against women, and Guatemala isn't far behind.[21] Femicide and domestic violence are some of the main drivers of the migration of women and children from the Northern Triangle, and gang members are major perpetrators. Yet women are woefully under-protected. A 2017 national survey found that 67 percent of Salvadoran women report suffering violence, be it domestic abuse or sexual assault outside the home. Yet only 6 percent of victims had reported abuse or assault to the government, with others saying that they were told under threat not to do so, or that they doubted the police would believe their accusations, or that they didn't know where to turn for help.[22]

ADRIANA

Since the murder of Brenda Paz, women are hardly ever initiated into Central American street gangs, and they are rarely found in leadership roles. Women are, however, always present in the families of gang members, often living with them. Most gang-affiliated women and girls work as low-level collaborators in their male family members' criminal enterprises. However, to discount the influence of these women simply because they lack official positions in the gang hierarchy seems to view the situation through the male gaze rather than through a more complex and realistic lens.

These women, much like the tens of thousands of male foot soldiers, aid and abet the gang. Members or not, they actively participate in many of the gang's criminal activities. Should we only consider women involved if they are leaders or if they can claim official membership, but not if they are wives or mothers or girlfriends? I don't know the answer to that question, but it seems to me that only looking at the gang through the prism of the overwhelmingly male initiated members and not as a whole within the networks in which they are housed is to fail to really understand the significance of women in these gangs. Without taking a broader view, we are marginalizing women and discounting their relationships and bonds to the male members, and how those bonds influence the gang and its existence. We are blind to the ways women influence decisions and dynamics within gangs, albeit from beneath if not from above. As investigator Juan José Martínez told me, if the male *ranfla* (top leadership of the gang) is the engine that keeps the car running, at least half of the rest of the car—the body, the exhaust system, the tires—is made up of women.

Even if the gangs are officially instructed not to allow women into the organization, some homegirls (the term for sanctioned members) remain in El Salvador. Gang members and experts I interviewed during the research for this book told me that, although it's rare, women are still initiated into the gangs at the discretion of individual cliques. Adriana, whom I met in San Salvador, was one of those rare cases. Although she was only twenty-seven, her eyes were tired, her light-brown Afro pulled away from her face to show skin mottled by years of self-professed drug use. After her mother died of cancer when she was twelve, Adriana turned to embrace the only other family she would ever know, she told me: the Barrio 18.

"I started living on the streets. My brothers were older. I was always involved in that [gang] world, because of where we lived. My brothers always smoked weed and drank, and I saw all this, and when I got to a certain age, I wanted to do it too, to be around them. I was the only girl, and I always liked being with the boys." Adriana spoke in a low mumble, and I had to keep asking her to repeat things to be sure that I understood what she was saying.

"The homeboys knew me from such a young age that they respected me. They started to see that I wasn't like the *hainas* [girlfriends] who hung out with them—those women gave them love. I wasn't like that. I sold weed, I did jobs, and bit by bit I started getting more involved in the gang."[23]

Eventually Adriana was jumped into the gang, despite the nationwide ban. "Four guys did it," she said. "They didn't rape me the way that they did the majority of other young girls, which is what they used to do between 2001 and 2008. When I entered in 2011, it was really rare, really rare, for them to jump women into the gang." She said that she chose the beating over the rape, and that it was the longest few minutes of her life.

"I was always in the game. On the lookout, selling weed, cocaine, crack. We stole cars—I learned how to steal cars and mug people. I always really liked the adrenaline—I liked being in the street, in the game. I loved it."

She was known as "La Tranki," she told me, "The Calm One." Her demeanor came in handy for the "missions" she ascended to, gang code for assassinations, usually of rival gang members. "It's so much adrenaline," she said. "I used to do it when I was high, because it's when I had more courage. You have to find the courage one way or the other. It feels bad the first time, yeah, but then after the second, third or fourth time, it felt like something routine. You tell yourself once you've done it once, you can do it again."

Adriana was *calmada* (inactive) when I met her in November 2021. She and the male gang member who introduced me to her said that they had lost count of the number of people they had killed. But I sensed, speaking to her, that Adriana was proud of her acceptance into the male world of Barrio 18. But it felt to me that even though she had ascended to a significant level in the gang, her power and approval still depended overwhelmingly on the men around her, and she was moving very much within a male organism.

Her pride in her place in the gang made me wonder how she saw her life compared with how it looked from outside. For me, understanding her circumstances made the illogical seem logical. Following her mother's death, Adriana's brothers had abandoned her, she said, leaving her alone on the streets. That's when she started working for the gang. Barrio 18 was survival to her, what she perceived to be her safest option among a few pretty limited choices. Might I have done the same in her position?

I grew up in a world with parents there to love me, siblings there to look up to me, and teachers there to school me. But what I could understand—as a woman and an immigrant whose parents moved to a new city every five years, as someone who never wanted to draw too much attention to herself or stand out—was the need to belong. I understood why Adriana felt utterly alone and sought a sense of belonging where she could find it. Orphaned and abandoned, she needed a group, a family, in which to root herself. I think that this is why gangs prove such a lure to so many men and women across the Americas, who feel let down or betrayed by their own families or shut out by the communities around them. That, and the thrill of the power and adrenaline gang life offers to the most maligned and disempowered group in the region: poor, disenfranchised, largely brown men and women.

Adriana's pride put her above the women who "gave love" in the gangs, the *hainas* who slept with or went out with male gang members.

"Because most women are hainas, and hainas snitch," said Adriana.

———

Juan, another gang member I interviewed in November 2021, provided additional insight into how things used to be for women when there were more homegirls around. We spoke in the back garden of a suburban house in El Salvador on a weekday afternoon. I could see the blue hint of the tattoos underneath the makeup that caked his face in an attempt to conceal them. Male gang members like him who have done time in jail plaster their face tattoos with foundation before they leave the house to avoid being singled out by the police. Juan couldn't remember how many people he had killed, but he had served more than two decades in prison for some of those murders. He agreed to meet me and my companions in our car at a busy intersection some way from his home before traveling to the house for the interview.

By the time we met he had spent twenty years as an active member of Barrio 18, much of it in prison, but he was now "calmada," like Adriana. He was first initiated into the organization in the late 1990s via a homegirl who was known as Lovely. "I really liked her—she was a great woman. She was beautiful," Juan remembered. "She schooled me, she told me what I had to do. She told me this is done this way; you have to stand firm. You have to be firm—don't go back on what you talk about, on what you say. You mustn't be afraid—that's the worst enemy that you can have."

After a year of being schooled by Lovely, he was jumped into the gang. "When I got jumped in, she started to move away from me." Her role had been to train and evaluate him, and her work was done.[24]

ESMERALDA

Esmeralda Aravel Flores Acosta drove up to the curb in front of the local registry office in the small town of Santa Ana, an hour outside San Salvador, scanning the sidewalk with her eyes. When she spotted a man standing outside the government building that issued marriage licenses, she pointed. "There's your husband," she said joylessly to an apprehensive-looking woman in the back seat.

She ordered the passenger, Monica, to get out of the car. Monica, who worked for Esmeralda caring for her children, did what her boss told her. Esmeralda watched as Monica approached the man and took his hand. They didn't speak.

It was the only time in her adult life that Monica had taken the hand of a man she'd never met before. Esmeralda had made a deal with him, Melvin Ostmaro Reyes Rosa, thirty-one, a chubby day laborer. He believed that he was marrying Monica to get the paperwork he needed for the right to live and work in the US—a dream for many impoverished Salvadorans. There was one condition: that he take out a life insurance policy.

Reyes Rosa didn't know that day in September 2016 that not only did Monica not have a US passport, but when he married her, he would be signing away his life. Esmeralda had lied to him about just about everything. Monica (whose real name was withheld in court documents to protect her identity) wasn't a US citizen as Esmeralda had claimed. The insurance policy wasn't needed as part of the visa application she had said she would help Reyes Rosa complete. There would be no visa application.

Just over a month after the civil ceremony that he and Monica underwent that day, at a bus stop not far from where they were wed, Reyes Rosa was shot dead by members of MS-13. The killers tried to make the murder look like a random robbery by taking Reyes Rosa's phone and wallet, but there was nothing unplanned about it. His unholy union with Monica and his subsequent murder were the results of an elaborate scheme hatched by a human trafficking ring led by Esmeralda with two of her sisters and a couple of her female friends. These women were backed by the muscle and terror of MS-13. Their objective? To force women to marry men the gang would later kill so that the group could claim the insurance money.[25]

The Black Widow, as Esmeralda came to be called by the local press, took the role of a woman in a gang to an entirely new level. "Esmeralda not only established a criminal enterprise, but she established a working relationship with one of the most misogynist, powerful criminal enterprises in the region [MS-13]. I've never seen a woman like that here in El Salvador," said gang expert Martínez.[26]

Little is known about Esmeralda outside her role in the human trafficking scheme, other than that she was a former hairdresser and divorced with at least two children. She was thirty-seven at the time she formed the Black Widows, and stills from video sessions during her trial show a striking woman with jet-black hair and dark eyes.

What I know about her criminal side I learned mostly from poring over documents with my local colleague and journalist Bryan Avelar in a government office in San Salvador. The government workers gave us permission to read and photograph more than thirty thick folders of information, and doing so made me feel as though I were in the cast of the film *Spotlight*. This was old school! Court documents that I had accessed through the US justice system were always online and digital, read from the comfort of my desk at home.

The painstaking process was worth the hassle, though, because buried in those documents was real gold. They contained photos of notebooks seized from Esmeralda's house, which were filled with details about the group's spending listed in order of items, cost, and for whom the purchases were made. She was meticulous and ran her house like a tight ship: a house full of women she regularly beat with a wooden bat.

I was never able to speak to Esmeralda. Requests to visit and interview her in prison were denied by the Bukele administration in El Salvador, under the pretext of COVID-19 restrictions, despite the fact that the pandemic had subsided by 2022. But Sonja Wolf of CIDE, who follows the gangs closely, cautioned against assuming Esmeralda was a powerful ringleader acting independently, given the track record of women in Mara cells. "Even if some women have ostensibly adopted the role of a victimizer, they may themselves have been victimized, and this experience may be important to explain how they come to victimize others," said Wolf. "If [Esmeralda] Flores was in a relationship with a clique leader, to what extent might she be seen as another victim in the Black Widows scheme, rather than a ringleader?"[27]

I can only speculate how much agency Esmeralda had in her life, but her leadership style is an outlier and not representative of the role of the women in gangs today. No matter how comfortable she was with violence, Esmeralda was tense following the murder of Reyes Rosa. Experience told her that Monica had to get the right documents and be a convincing widow in order to claim the life insurance from the local bank. She told Monica to go to the police station to report that her man was a womanizer, but that she was worried about him because he hadn't been home for days.

When police investigators found Reyes Rosa's body, his face was horribly deformed by the attack. According to the autopsy report, he had been shot in the face and the back of the head, as well as in his abdomen, left shoulder, thigh, and knee. When Esmeralda sent Monica to the local morgue to identify the body, she struggled to recognize him but recalled to investigators that the clothes he was wearing when he was killed were ones he had worn in her company.[28]

As Esmeralda made the burial arrangements, she warned Monica that during the funeral she had to play the grieving widow. It would be ideal if she cried and, if possible, passed out. Monica obliged, according to her own testimony.[29]

Eventually, Monica got the call from the bank to tell her that the check for the life insurance money was waiting for her. When she overheard the call, Esmeralda jumped up and down with delight, clapping her hands, telling Monica that she had done a "great job."[30] But it wasn't the job she had originally agreed to do for Esmeralda.

Monica first met the Black Widow when Esmeralda offered her live-in domestic work in July 2016 through a mutual friend. Monica had no work at the time, she later told prosecutors, so she decided to try it out for a monthly salary of $250, which was below the minimum wage.[31] She moved in with Esmeralda, Esmeralda's young children, and their mutual friend, Magdalena Patricia Lucha López. But one day Monica glimpsed Magdalena in the shower and saw that her back was full of bruises—evidence, she told prosecutors, of what she thought were beatings from Esmeralda. Frightened, Monica decided to invent a story to leave the job. She told Esmeralda that a member of her family had fallen sick and that she needed to return home to look after them. "OK," her boss replied.[32]

The next day, Esmeralda asked Monica, before she left for home, to help her take a plate of food to a house on the next block. As they walked past the house's front window, Monica saw a tall and muscular man inside with tattoos covering every inch of his skin, including his face. The only part of him not covered in ink was his hands. Monica knew that those tattoos were a declaration of the man's membership and loyalty to MS-13. The man was Wilbur Javier Caceres Benitez, or "El Guay" ("Whitey"). Esmeralda was in a sexual relationship with him at the time and outsourced her terror tactics to him.

As they walked through the door, the man pounced on Monica and put a gun to her head. She dropped the plate of food in her hand, and it smashed on the tiled floor. "You're going to do exactly what Esmeralda tells you to do, and if not, we're going to kill your whole family—your mother, your sister, and your son; we have photos of all of them," he said through gritted teeth as he stared at her with yellowed eyes.

"Why are you doing this to me?" Monica said.

Esmeralda told Monica that they wanted her to do a job for them, and then they would let her go. She told Monica that she would explain everything as they went along but that she wouldn't be let go until the job was done. "The only response to this is yes or yes," she finished before smacking Monica in the face.[33]

Monica knew she was trapped in Esmeralda's web. After she married Reyes Rosa and he was killed, she reported him missing to the police and played the grieving widow at his wake, as she was ordered to do. Monica then claimed his body and later his life insurance payments—money that she subsequently turned over to Esmeralda.

From Monica's marriage alone, Esmeralda and her collaborators made more than $60,000, according to court documents—a small fortune in El Salvador, where almost a quarter of families live below the poverty line.[34] In another marriage allegedly forced onto another female victim named in the official documents only as "Mateo," the Black Widows also killed the husband and forced Mateo to claim his life insurance payments, as well as a $150 pension every month.[35]

Monica said in court that she was never paid a cent by Esmeralda. Instead, Esmeralda beat her and the other women in the house with a heavy wooden bat. It wasn't until Monica was claiming her dead husband's insurance money that she realized her captor had no intention of letting her go home to her family once the job was done. The bank that gave her the payout wanted to give her a free life insurance policy. When Esmeralda asked Monica if she had signed up for it, she replied that she didn't have all the necessary documents at the time, and Esmeralda flew into a rage. That's when Monica understood she was next on her boss's hit list. That Esmeralda planned to force Monica's mother to claim the insurance money after Esmeralda had her killed too.

On a day in late January 2017, Esmeralda told Monica to see her family and tell them she was never coming back. But when Monica left the house that day, she did nothing of the sort. Instead, she finally went to the police with all of the evidence she had collected over the last year with Esmeralda. She gave them copies of Reyes Rosa's death certificate, their marriage documents, the insurance payouts, as well as photos of herself covered in bruises from the beatings from Esmeralda. Added to that were death threats left by Esmeralda on Monica's phone when she realized Monica had gone AWOL.[36]

Esmeralda went underground, abandoning the house shortly before it was raided by the police. The police rescued the other women who had been held captive there. Three of them later testified to the same treatment that Monica described—one had been held captive for three years.

It wasn't until ten months later, in November 2017, that Esmeralda was finally arrested. In May 2019, she was sentenced to thirty years in prison, going down in ignoble history as the first case of forced marriage on Salvadoran record.

———

The stories in this chapter convinced me that the role of women in Central America's street gangs is underestimated and misunderstood. Their power is present and nuanced but often unseen unless they're violent protagonists—a problem that runs through our understanding of women in organized crime as a whole.

Meeting Adriana and Isabel, and digging into the cases of Brenda and Esmeralda provided me with a peek inside the world of gang-affiliated women beyond the narrative of the victim and gave me a taste of the deeper insight to be had.

I still long to meet Esmeralda, to hear her talk of her criminal enterprise in her own words. Were there motivations other than money behind her actions? Is she remorseful? Does she regret victimizing the men and women she needed to use in order to defraud the life insurance companies? What is her relationship to the gang, and what was the nature of her romance with one of its enforcers, Wilbur? Was she under his spell? Was he under hers? The nature of power within sexual and romantic relationships is complex, but it seemed to me that their union was the nexus via which her violent criminal enterprise operated. I wanted to know whose idea the forced-marriage plan had been, and how much of the initiative behind it came from Esmeralda herself.

Like so many of the women in this book, Esmeralda may never speak to me—either as a result of her own decision or the government's determination to keep her out of the limelight. The voices of women from the criminal underworld are so rarely heard that many of the questions around their crimes remain unanswered, leaving space for supposition, speculation, and pure fiction.

But sometimes I have been lucky during my fieldwork, finding myself face to face with the women at the center of these stories.

CHAPTER 5

THE LEMUS SISTERS AND THE BATTLE FOR MOYUTA

SANTA TERESA

There is an entire ecosystem outside the Santa Teresa prison in Guatemala City that caters to the needs and desires of those on the inside. People who come to visit their family or friends here are a lifeline. They bring in the things that in other regions the state is expected to provide: sanitary napkins, tampons, toothpaste and toothbrushes, toilet paper, soap, shampoo, sugar, ketchup, chips, cookies, combs, eggs, water, blankets, disposable plates and cups, nuts, and wipes.

Many visitors come from far away, and rather than carry those items the entire journey, they buy them when they arrive, at stalls specially built for this purpose on the road up to the prison. The improvised shops have wood walls and corrugated iron roofs. Everything for sale is piled up unceremoniously inside, as though each stall were a storage room.

Bathroom cubicles concealed by filthy hanging curtains offer visitors a final chance for the toilet before having to wait in line to get into the prison. The wait can be long, from twenty minutes to a few hours. It is also where many women take the opportunity to change their clothes. The modest outfits they wear for the bus ride to the prison are replaced by the clothes they want their men inside to see them wearing. There seems to be almost a uniform: very short, tight stretchy dresses that barely cover their butt cheeks, and Greek-style sandals with thin soles and string straps that wrap in a crisscross pattern up their ankles and lower calves. Women wear these outfits regardless of their shape or weight. They're owning it.

The final approach to the gates of the prison is up a steep hill, and for a few pesos, sweaty men run wheelbarrows up the hill full of the goods that people—overwhelmingly women—have bought outside the prison to take inside. Many of the women have young children on their hips, and they either follow the wheelbarrow men up the hill slowly or pay a few more pesos to ride the rest of the way in a tuktuk—a three-wheeled motorcycle taxi.

Many of the women are coming to see boyfriends, brothers, or husbands who are members of the Mara Salvatrucha or Barrio 18 street gangs, according to my local contact, whom we'll call Iris. Iris spends a lot of time in and around Santa Teresa. She tells me that women wear these outfits for two reasons. One is that it's the gang style, believed to complement the baggy pants, vests, and cholo style that their men favor.

But the second reason is that all of the women who pass into the prison are subjected to full body searches, as described by Isabel in chapter 4. Vaginas and anuses are the perfect carrying space for drugs, money rolls, and even small weapons. Criminal enterprises are run out of prisons like this one. Drug and extortion rackets thrive, and women play a fundamental role in bringing things in and out. The short dresses speed up the body searches, a deeply undignified process for the guards as well as the girlfriends, wives, and mothers coming in.

"You can get used to anything," Isabel said about the searches. Like Isabel, those visiting people in *poblacion*—which means "population" and is shorthand for the general area of the prison—see the body searches as a necessary evil.

I was at Santa Teresa to visit a woman in solitary confinement, in an area designated high security due to the nature of its inmates.

Her name was Marixa Lemus, and she had already escaped from jail twice, earning herself the moniker of Guatemala's "female Chapo," after the Mexican drug lord who made several cinematic jail breaks. She was now being held in solitary to avoid the embarrassment of yet another escape. Her past two jailbreaks had earned her celebrity status, which was the main reason I didn't seek official journalist's permission to enter the prison and talk with her. I was certain the government would reject such a request.

That's why Iris was smuggling me in under the guise of working for her. As the women in the tiny dresses and sandals filed into the building, we had to wait for the prison director to show up to sign a permission form with my name on it.

"I'm going to do the talking. You just listen," Iris said as we waited. And when the prison director showed up, I did as I had been told, standing silently as he signed the form. My body search was mercifully brief, and they did allow me to take a pen and paper into the prison. We followed a guard down a slope into the high-security part of the women's prison, which had been broken into sections using wire fences. Women sat around in small groups, some of them brushing each other's hair or playing cards.

I had no idea what most of the women in this section of the prison were in for. Latin America's female prison population has surged in the last two decades to "alarming proportions," not just in numbers but as a percentage of the overall number of people incarcerated in the region. As of 2018, many of the countries in this region have a higher percentage of female prison populations than the global average.[1]

The rate of growth for the number of women behind bars has overtaken that of men. The use of pretrial detention as a default for most Latin American countries means that many women are stuck in the penitentiary system for years, waiting for their judicial process to grind into motion. In the case of Guatemalan prisons like the Santa Teresa, the female population has grown sixfold, from 433 behind bars in 2001 to 2,923 in prison in 2020.[2]

Few women are in prison on charges as serious as Marixa's. Although women in Latin America are increasingly involved in organized crime, such as the drug trade, the vast majority of them are arrested and incarcerated for low-level offenses, such as growing plants that are processed to produce street drugs, such as coca (a plant that is the base ingredient for cocaine and is grown and harvested in South America), poppy (which produces opium and heroin), and marijuana. Women in the drug trade also often work as mules or street sellers, crimes that are often punished harshly in Latin American countries. These low-level offenses are the biggest drivers in the growth of female incarceration, according to a recent study.[3]

The social and economic impact of so many women behind bars is sobering, and it has an impact not just on the present moment but on the future development of society. Single-parent families are so common in countries like Guatemala that women are often the sole caregivers and earners for their children. With them inside, the money dries up. In most prisons, women are allowed to have their children with them until they're three or four years old, which isn't an ideal solution but is preferable for many mothers to the alternative: leaving their kids with relatives or friends on the outside. But women behind bars have little choice but to leave their older children to fend for themselves in a country where the lure of drugs, crime, and gangs is on nearly every street corner.

Some of you may be thinking that mothers probably shouldn't get involved in transporting or trafficking drugs, even small amounts. Stigma around women's involvement in the drug trade exists not only because of the ethical questions around the drug trade itself and what it does to communities, but because women often choose to participate. And it happens with much more frequency than one might think.

I can only report on what I have seen in many Latin American communities, which is a high level of poverty partnered with a lack of better options for many people. Some women choose to go the illegal route and get involved in the drug trade, while some don't. Why? These are the big questions in life—how humans make different choices when confronted with the same set of circumstances. For all of the women in prison who don't get away with their crimes, there are many women who actually do, and their criminal activities provide an income for them and their families that they can't—or don't want to—earn elsewhere.

In my research I've found that some women are attracted to this kind of work, just as some men are. "Brenda," the woman serving time for running a kidnapping ring whom I mentioned in the introduction, said she was "curious about how things were done" when I asked why she got involved in the business.

She was a fairly major player in the crime stakes, but the vast majority of incarcerated women are doing time for much smaller offenses. Most are not what constitutes a "danger to society." Many, when released, will likely feel forced to turn to the same means to survive that got them arrested in the first place. It is a depressing, vicious cycle that cannot stop unless one of the founding pillars of the drug war—punitive laws for low-level drug offenses that overwhelmingly affect women—change or even disappear.

That day at Santa Teresa, many of the women I passed to get to Marixa were in there for the long haul. Iris and I followed the guard into a small building that felt like a house, where we exchanged niceties with the director of the female section. No one asked me who I was or what I was doing there.

Next door to the female section director's room was a "cell," which was in fact a room. There were no bars. In it stood Roxana Baldetti, Guatemala's former, now-disgraced vice president. Iris greeted her and casually introduced us.

You may remember Roxana from chapter 3. She was allegedly one of Marllory Chacón's high-powered contacts and enablers—something Roxana has always denied. Marllory, the money launderer and trafficker who worked with Sebastiana Cottón Vásquez and Yaneth

Vergara Hernández, had been through the US justice system by the time I met Roxana in 2020. Marllory's time inside may have had something to do with the fact that there were now drug trafficking charges awaiting Roxana in the US. Her extradition—once she had served the fifteen-year sentence she got for corruption in Guatemala—was pretty much guaranteed.

I have written thousands of words about Roxana and the charges against her and the sitting president at the time, Otto Pérez Molina. Their story is part of a crucial chapter in Guatemalan history, during which street protests and an international investigation into a kickback scheme displaced both of them. Roxana is a criminal celebrity, and suddenly I was face to face with her.

She had her hair pulled back into a ponytail, gray showing among the black. She was calm and yet animated and in good spirits, despite her reduced circumstances. I was glad she didn't know I was a journalist. As with everyone else in Santa Teresa, she didn't ask who I was or what I was doing in the high-security wing. Instead, she showed us the baby dolls she had been making and packaging up for sale on the outside. I spotted an Apple laptop sitting on her perfectly made bed, which was in a bedroom separate from her living space. I wondered if it had an internet connection.

Roxana was, at that point, perhaps Guatemala's most high-profile prisoner. And Marixa Lemus was being held in the same wing.

MEETING LA PATRONA

Marixa, now in her late forties, came up some stairs from a basement cell into the bright atrium where I was waiting for her. She blinked as she emerged from the dark wing. She wore a white Nike cap over long thick black hair pulled back into a ponytail. Her skin was pale and clear, with a hint of freckles, her brows thick and dark. She was wearing a black Adidas T-shirt over a white long-sleeved top.

I explained to her that I was writing a book about women in organized crime and that I wanted to interview her. She hadn't had any warning about my visit, but she immediately sat down at a table in the corner to speak with me as prison guards and inmates idled past. She wanted to tell me her story. I hadn't been allowed to bring in a recording device, so I was focused on writing down everything she said. I was told we'd have twenty minutes.

By the time we met, I had been to the Guatemala–El Salvador border region of the Jutiapa department where she grew up with her sister Mayra, her brother Magno, and the rest of the Lemus clan. Most of her closest family members were now gone after a deadly fight for political and criminal power. Marixa was a survivor.

Her stomping ground was a key corridor for drugs moving north and drug profits moving south. The Lorenzana family, whom you might remember from chapter 3, dominated the main corridor, on the southeastern Guatemala border with Honduras. Jutiapa, in the southwest part of Guatemala, is home to major highways that cross over from El Salvador. When I drove into Ciudad de Pedro Alvarado, which Marixa used to control, a couple of weeks before visiting her in jail, the road that crossed the international line was packed with huge container trucks bumper to bumper, waiting to cross south into El Salvador. From the other side, trucks drove from El Salvador into Guatemala.

Drug trafficking cartels and their accomplices use the constant movement of legal goods on borders like these to hide their product in plain sight. Packaged cocaine and heroin are often hidden in compartments or packed between products such as sugar and beans. Drugs being trafficked by women like Digna Valle, Marllory Chacón, and Sebastiana Cottón further south in Central America, and Guadalupe Fernández and Luz Fajardo to the north in Mexico, likely passed through this crucial gateway. Locals and the anti-narcotics prosecutors in Guatemala City argue that there are simply too many trucks to check and search. Border authorities in countries such as these rarely have enough working scanners and agents to carry out even basic revisions of trucks and containers coming through. Both police and local residents say that the drugs move north, and the cash profits from their sale are concealed in trucks to be transported back to suppliers in South America.[4]

The illegal products constantly moving through this pipeline are what makes border cities like these such lucrative territory. Local authorities, elected or not, can help or hinder the precious cargo moving through, and they can tax regional organizations such as those run by the Lorenzanas to the east, the Valles to the South, and the El Chapos to the north to ensure safe passage.

But there is only room for one Patrón—or Patrona, as Marixa came to be known following her arrest. And in the town of Moyuta, which is right next to the border town of Ciudad de Pedro Alvarado, the fight for power became a blood sport.

The Lemus family to which Marixa belonged had a legacy of political power in the town, as well as a history of affiliating with regional narco organizations bringing drugs up from other parts of Central America. Her clan controlled the valued border crossing, one of the gateways for traffickers moving product farther north into Guatemala and closer to the United States.

Almost on top of that border crossing is a hotel called Los Cuernos. Hundreds of container trucks rumble past it each day. It was here that Mayra, Marixa's older sister, ate her final meal in February 2011. She was running for mayor of Moyuta in the approaching local election and brought some of her supporters together for a campaign lunch.

The attendees had barely finished their entrées when two pickup trucks pulled up to the hotel. Heavily armed men jumped out. They raised their AK-47 rifles and opened fire before the diners could react, according to witnesses. They gunned down eight people that day, including Mayra and at least one of her bodyguards.

Marixa, who was down the road at a local horse festival at the time, told me she heard the gunfire start. She jumped into her armored truck and raced toward the fray. Her bodyguards leapt into another truck to follow her, honking the horn, trying to warn her to stop. But Marixa was set on getting to her sister.

When the gunmen at the hotel saw her truck coming down the road, they turned their weapons in her direction and started spraying bullets. Marixa could feel and hear the rounds pinging off her windscreen. She knew she had to stop. She screeched her truck to a halt and flung it into reverse.

She told me that she went straight to the local police, but they refused to get involved. By the time Marixa returned cautiously to the hotel, the armed men were long gone. And so was Mayra. She found her sister's body in a back office a few meters away from where she had been having lunch. Mayra had crawled there to hide, but her aggressors had fired through the door and barged in. "Her face was destroyed, and she was lying in a pool of her own blood," Marixa told me.

The attack is now the stuff of local legend and ten years later is known as "the massacre at Los Cuernos." But Mayra's murder that day wasn't completely unexpected. "She was famous for being a killer. The whole town was scared of her because she was a killer. It's that simple. She decided who lived and who died," a local business owner told me as we spoke in the shade of the Los Cuernos restaurant. Mayra was killed just a few feet from the table where we sat talking.

Local legend has it that Mayra, who in photos has shoulder-length red hair and a stocky build, killed her own husband in their house and then dumped his body in another part of town. I could not verify this event, and she was never charged or convicted for it. But ten years after her death, the fear of her was still palpable in the people I spoke with about her.

In part, her power in the town was derived from geography and context. If you're entrenched in illegal business, such as the drug trade, protecting territory or market share is a simple equation: kill or be killed. It's not that the business is full of psychopaths with a bloodlust (although there are those), but violence is a business strategy, a tool that protects territory and markets and creates terror to keep people submissive to your will. Mayra understood that, as did her siblings.

"I can't tell you how many holes she had in her body that day," Marixa said of her sister. "I saw her back. I knew she was dead." Her eyes filled with tears.

When she was killed, Mayra was one of only two contenders for the prize of mayor. Her brother Magno had been mayor of Moyuta until he died in 2009 of a heart attack. Mayra was had replaced him and was finishing his term as she ran for election. But it wasn't the first time that someone had tried to get rid of her—and Magno.

A few minutes' drive from the Hotel Los Cuernos, the road weaves to the right and then the left as it rises out of Ciudad Pedro de Alvarado. An arch-shaped shrine sits to the side of the highway, almost invisible because of the long grass. There are three rusting crosses underneath the arch, with the names of the dead daubed in white underneath, all Lemuses. There is a stump where a fourth cross used to be: it bore the name of Marixa's daughter, Jennifer, age nineteen, who was among those killed here in 2006. A gunman opened fire on the car Jennifer was traveling in with her aunt Mayra and uncle Magno. But since the memorial was installed, someone had yanked that cross out of the ground.

Both Mayra and Magno survived the highway ambush, which occurred during another political campaign: Magno's first run for mayor. He went on to win the election he and Mayra were campaigning for, and the author of that highway attack remains opaque. But, Marixa thinks she knows who is responsible for the massacre at the Hotel Los Cuernos restaurant that killed Mayra: Roberto Marroquín Fuentes, the Lemuses' political nemesis.

Marroquín, who at the time of writing this book is still the mayor of Moyuta—was Mayra's political rival in the election race in 2011 and one of the main suspects in the investigation into her killing that happened months before the vote, according to reports based on documents from Guatemala's prosecutor's office. When Mayra was killed, Marixa stepped into her warm shoes in the election race.[5]

To improve her chances of winning, she built a coalition with another political (and criminal) rival of Marroquín's, a man named

Rony Rodríguez, who was the candidate with the best chance of beating Marroquín in the vote for mayor. Media reports also claimed that Rodríguez had inherited more from Magno than just his political mantle: following Magno's death, it was now Rodríguez who was taxing the drug routes.

Rodríguez's political bid wasn't to be. He was gunned down a few months after Mayra, leaving Marixa to campaign alone for the election. Marroquín won in a landslide.

Marixa hates Marroquín with the kind of burning passion that I could warm my hands on as I sat next to her in Santa Teresa prison. So much so that, according to Marroquín, she tried to kill him. Three times.

The alleged assassination attempts took place within the space of six months. Gunmen ambushed the car in which Marroquín was traveling in November 2013, and less than a month later, bombs were planted on a bridge that he had to cross on his drive home, according to local media reports. The bombs never exploded, and local police, who were allegedly in on the plot, ran off, leaving their AK-47s and at least one grenade on the scene to be found later by investigators.

The third attempt happened when Marixa was already behind bars. The list of crimes she had been detained for was grim. She and seven other alleged accomplices were arrested by the National Police in April 2014, accused of kidnapping and subsequently killing Marixa's aunt, Amanda Lemus. Marixa and her gang had abducted Amanda and demanded a $30,000 ransom for her, according to Guatemala's Public Ministry.[6] Even after I talked with Marixa, it wasn't clear to me what her motive was for abducting and killing her aunt, but it's possible Marixa had information that led her to believe her relative's loved ones could pay a ransom of that size.

In the statement following her arrest, the Public Ministry also connected Marixa with the second attempt on Marroquín's life in December 2013, as well as the murder of her own husband—Álvaro Alfonso Mejía Estrada—in February 2014.[7] The authorities alleged that she had him killed because she wanted to take control of some of the businesses that he owned. Despite her denials, Marixa was eventually condemned to a sobering 135 years behind bars for kidnapping and homicide.

But Marroquín still believes that Marixa was behind the third and final attempt on his life, despite being behind bars at the time it happened. Armed assailants injured him, his wife, and his bodyguard in November 2014 when his convoy was ambushed. It's not inconceivable that Marixa ordered the hit from prison, but many of the members of her gang had been arrested with her in April of that year, so finding the people to do for her as she sat in a jail cell would have been challenging.

Of course, I had to speak to Marroquín. Not just to give him the right to reply but also out of sheer curiosity to meet someone who had so bedeviled and perhaps even outsmarted Marixa. I watched him in TV interviews and looked up articles about him in the local press. He was small and slight, with close-cut black hair. He had a broad winning smile and a gregarious style and charm.

But when I was in Guatemala, my sources advised me not to meet with Marroquín in person. Some of those sources were officials themselves. It wasn't the first time in Latin America that I have seen people fear local governors and politicians more than they do narcos. It makes sense. Drug traffickers like the Lorenzanas, the Valles, or El Chapo have nowhere to hide—all they do is what they do. But politicians who are corrupt or doubling up and generating criminal profits on the side wear a cloak of legitimacy. They are harder to incriminate and discredit, and they arguably have more to lose if that happens. But impunity is the norm for officials who criminally offend, in this region, and they also have public resources—law enforcement, weapons, and government money—at their disposal to protect and further their interests.

"Before, it wasn't the narco who would run for mayor; the narcos would finance campaigns and pick the candidate. Now, mayors are running the drug trade directly," Gerson Alegría, Guatemala's chief anti–drug trafficking prosecutor, told me. He has seen arrests and evidence against locally elected officials mount as organized crime works with, not against, local elected powers. When I asked him about the tensions between the Lemus and Marroquín clans, he told me, "We have the same info: that it is a battle over territorial control."[8]

But neither Alegría's team nor any other part of the Guatemalan justice machinery has charged Marroquín with any crime.

I decided to err on the side of caution. I requested a Zoom call with Marroquín when I was back in Mexico City. He seemed delighted to oblige. We both appeared to enjoy our conversation thoroughly, despite the fact that I was asking him rather awkward questions about whether he'd ever tried to kill anyone.

Marroquín had nothing to do with Mayra's murder, he assured me, and said that he'd cooperated with the subsequent investigation. He has only ever acted to defend himself, he said, and the Lemus family resented him for his local popularity. Marroquín said he is a victim of a political establishment that wants to be rid of him because of his influence and good deeds. "If I was a narco, I wouldn't be a politician; I'd be in hiding," he told me from behind his desk in Moyuta, where, dressed in a dark blue shirt, he chuckled and gesticulated wildly.[9]

But a political career is the perfect cover for someone in the drug trade. Because who would have the audacity, right?

———

It's unclear whether Marroquín had anything to do with Marixa's arrest. But he couldn't forget about her even if he wanted to. Her two prison escapes since her arrest in 2014 have earned her attention, notoriety, and more jail time. The first time she escaped was in May 2016, two years after she was first arrested. Fellow prisoners reportedly helped her vault over a wall. She was captured again within hours. Undeterred, she tried again a year later, this time breaking out of the maximum-security Mariscal Zavala military prison, reportedly wearing a guard's uniform. A waiting car whisked her away. When the authorities finally caught her two weeks later, she was in neighboring El

Salvador. Photos on social media showed she had dyed her hair a dark red, like that of her sister Mayra. Her capture was a media sensation: even the president at the time, Jimmy Morales, tweeted about it.[10]

Knowing that she could escape made it hard for Marroquín to relax. "He shakes in his pants when he sees Marixa," a source in Ciudad de Pedro Alvarado told me. "He behaves like the big man when he moves around with his bodyguards, but he is very afraid of her. When she got out for the second time, he didn't leave his house until she was caught—didn't do a single public act."

Maybe he had other things on his mind? Almost at the same time Marixa was carrying out her second great escape, Marroquín's brother was also making history. Jorge Mario Marroquín Fuentes was caught in May 2017 with nearly a ton of cocaine in a boat off the coast of Acajutla, Sonsonate, San Salvador, a two-hour drive south across the border from Moyuta. El Salvador's minister of defense said at the time that it was the biggest cocaine seizure in the country, bar none.[11]

When I told Marixa that Marroquín had reportedly not left the house following news of her second escape, she didn't even bother to try to hide a broad smile. "I know [Marroquín] is terrified of me because I'm a woman who took the reins and I'm going to avenge myself and all of the family that he took away from me," she said. Marroquín is not what he appears, she said, and has cheated and tricked his way through life. She posits that there is another explanation for the attempts on his life. "They were *auto-atentados*," she said, suggesting that the "attacks" on his life were staged—by him. Another source in Ciudad Pedro Alvarado said the same thing, and when I repeated the theory to Alan Ajiatas, the deputy at the anti-narcotics prosecutor's office, he replied, "Well, as a result of the attempts on his life, [Marroquín] did justify buying bulletproof cars [with government money], so it's probable."[12]

Marroquín laughed when I shared the theory with him. But Marixa, who remained behind bars, wasn't laughing. "When I got out of Mariscal, he said that I was a dangerous woman and that he had to double his security. He came out talking and staining my family's name when he is himself involved [in these bad things]," she said.

So far, Marroquín still gets the last laugh. When I left Marixa in prison that day after our conversation in March 2021, she was clutching a folder of documents that she said were related to an appeal she was filing to get her sentence shortened. Nearly anything is possible in Latin American justice systems, but even so, the likelihood of her getting out anytime soon—legally or illegally—is slim.

I wish we had had more time to speak. I could have sat there listening to her stories for hours. A few weeks after I left Guatemala, someone named Mari Perez reached out to me via Facebook. I first saw the message, bleary-eyed, when I woke up in the morning. Since then, I have stopped checking my phone so early, in order to gather my wits before I do anything stupid.

"Hola—you were in Guatemala," said Perez.

"Yes," I answered. Then I looked at the photos on her profile, all of which were photos of Marixa.

A couple of days later, "Mari" tried to call. I did not pick up.

"I'm a family member of Marixa who you visited in Guatemala," she wrote. "She wants to know if you can talk to her more about your book."

It was possible—no, probable—that Marixa had access to Facebook in solitary confinement in a high security prison. If the government was monitoring her, and they saw that I was corresponding with her, the best that could happen was that they wouldn't let me back into the country again. The worst that could happen was that I could get mistaken for a collaborator of sorts. My local contact, Iris, was furious that I had even replied once. So I never replied again, despite the fact that I was *dying* to do so.

CHAPTER 6

SINALOA, AND EMMA CORONEL'S BEGINNING, MIDDLE, AND END

She raises the gun to shoot. Her jet-black hair and flawless white skin are shielded by a wide-brimmed hat from the already-scorching early morning March sun in Sinaloa, Mexico. Her teeth bite into her full lower lip, which is painted bright red. Thick, white manicured fingernails rest on the top of the Glock handgun for a moment as she finds her aim. She steadies herself using her strong athletic legs, her rounded, firm rump tightening as her heels dig into the graveled ground.

Then she lowers her finger to the trigger and pulses it once to shoot, the gun kicking back in her outstretched arms. This is the first time she has fired a gun in her life, but on the target a few meters in front of her, the bullet hits the human silhouette straight in the throat.

This is how Emma Coronel, wife of Joaquín "El Chapo" Guzmán, learned to shoot.

When her husband was extradited from Mexico to the United States in January 2017 to face trial for the drug trafficking empire he built from humble beginnings in Badiraguato, Sinaloa, Emma knew she was on her own. It was time for her to learn how to protect herself.

It didn't matter that she had grown up in the mountains of Sinaloa. "No one here gave a shit that she was Chapo's wife once he was extradited," said a source who trained cartels in urban warfare.

Born in California Emma then grew up in Canelas, a small town in the state of Durango, which neighbors Sinaloa in Mexico. These are tiny towns, where everyone knows everyone, and where many generations of families grow up in the same pueblitos. That part of Mexico is known as the Golden Triangle, famous for the clandestine plots of heroin poppy and marijuana that pepper its mountain ranges. Their produce supplies the Sinaloa Cartel's drug business to the US.

The state of Sinaloa is different from the rest of Mexico. The eponymous cartel founded and headquartered there has for decades controlled vast swaths of territory, both cities and rural areas, and brought with it a set of values and customs that have seeped into the lifeblood of the people. Rural agricultural traditions have combined with a contemporary consumer "bling" culture that's now propagated and promoted via TikTok, YouTube, and Instagram. It's *narcocultura* (narco culture) but on steroids. To many of those who live there, drug traffickers are heroes. Legends. Benefactors.

There is a "chapel" in central Culiacán that is dedicated to Jesús Malverde, the narco's unofficial saint. A Robin Hood–type bandit whom locals visit to pray to and ask for favors. The white-tiled floor is surrounded by dark green tiled walls. In the center of the chapel is a small cave-like room in which the walls are plastered with photos of men, women, and children, as well as bills (both dollars and pesos), all attached with tape. A bust of Malverde stands in front of a kneeler, a splay of artificial flowers behind it. Many of the times I've visited, a musician plays melancholy songs to those at the chapel asking for favors. Visitors kneel in front of Malverde's bust, place a hand on his head, ask for what they need, and leave an offering in return.

Tourist mementos such as key rings, mugs, and imprinted candles bearing the image of Malverde as well as drug lord Joaquín "El Chapo" Guzmán have long been sold outside the chapel. But sometime in 2019, a new souvenir appeared in the small stalls outside the chapel: a perfectly sculpted statuette of Emma Coronel's husband, El Chapo, resplendent in a blue cap and pink shirt, with a plastic AK-47 in his hands, standing a diminutive forty centimeters tall.

El Chapo is the archetypal Sinaloan man. Rural, gruff, simple, brave, and strong. He uses his local knowledge and mastery of violence to overcome his rivals. *Un cabrón*, *pues*. A real bastard, but not always in a bad way. In Sinaloa's rural parts, a fiercely macho culture dictates that the men tend the animals and the land, while the responsibilities for the house and children fall to the women.

El Chapo's effigy for sale signals a broader trend—the commodification and exportation of narcocultura around the world, as his cartel has grown in strength and reach. Before, his image only appeared in the media. Now, it adorns caps and T-shirts and key rings. He is a well-known figure who, at least at home, is publicly worshipped as a hero by many. Of course, there are many more who reject this characterization, both in Sinaloa and elsewhere in Mexico. But his place in local legend is assured.

"We're like a big ranch with a Costco," Natalia Reyes, a feminist activist who grew up in Sinaloa, told me.[1] She was referring to the dangerous combination of rural conservative values and American consumerism that has grown in Sinaloa over the last five decades. This has occurred alongside the expanding demand for cocaine, methamphetamine, heroin—and, most recently, fentanyl—that gives drug trafficking corporations like the one El Chapo created such far-reaching power and influence.

Emma Coronel learned that being the wife of a powerful drug trafficker is rather like walking a tightrope. Everyone's eyes are on you, which is a massive thrill, but if you fall, the consequences can be deadly. Especially if there's no safety net.

If drug traffickers are heroes, their women are also to be worshipped and adored. Some part of Emma loved that. She was a daily presence at the trial of her husband in New York, which meant that her picture was plastered across the internet and newspapers as the case played out. She knew that people would recognize her wherever she went and that any anonymity she might have benefited from in the past was now lost. But maybe she didn't mind that, because perhaps Emma had always wanted to be a star. She must have known from the day in 2007 when she first met El Chapo on a dusty ranch dance floor in the tiny town of Canelas, when she was a seventeen-year-old aspiring beauty queen, that she might one day be the most famous woman in Sinaloa.

"He was dancing with another girl, I was dancing with my boyfriend, and we met right in the middle of the dance floor. He smiled at me, all flirty," Coronel remembered in an interview with Mexican journalist Anabel Hernández in 2016. "Then someone said to me, 'The señor has asked if you want to dance with him.' And I said, 'OK.'"[2]

It's quite a thing for a teenage girl to get involved with a man like El Chapo. By then, he was already the stuff of legend, having escaped, in 2001, his first maximum-security holding cell in a prison known as Puente Grande, allegedly by hiding in a laundry basket. When he met Coronel, he was already an outlaw, a legendary bandit loved by many for his rags-to-riches story. Swaths of Sinaloans consider him a benefactor to the humble poppy gum and marijuana farmers in his state, and many feel that drug traffickers provide employment and protection while the government doesn't. When President Andrés Manuel López Obrador visited Badiraguato, El Chapo's birthplace, in March 2020, he defied recently imposed COVID restrictions to shake the hand of El Chapo's mother as she sat in her car, a gesture that provoked both amusement and scorn.[3] Even the Mexican president acknowledges the drug lord's legacy.

Two years after meeting Coronel, El Chapo made his first appearance on the *Forbes* list of the richest people in the world, cementing his wealth and fame, and making him a catch for women in certain circles. Narco circles. Emma's father, Inés Coronel Barreras, was also a drug trafficker, and his daughter's close relationship with the drug lord was good for business. Emma had grown up around the narco life.

That day in Canelas, after they did the rounds on the dance floor, Chapo won Emma's hand in marriage, and she won the beauty contest. It was then that her tightrope walk began, with her emotional and financial involvement with Chapo. He was her safety net, but that would eventually be taken away.

Legend has it that Chapo made sure she won the beauty contest after they met dancing. That he sent in a cavalcade of men on motorbikes, armed with cash, to convince the judges—something Emma subsequently denied. And I believe her. Emma's beauty is undisputed in those circles. She didn't need his help. Today, her long straight dark hair and tiny waist, coupled with a prominent rump and bust, has become the archetype of a certain type of beauty, not just in Sinaloa but across Mexico.

That "look" has become aspirational.

LAS BUCHONAS

"I was in a hair salon once, and there was a young woman there getting hair extensions. She turned to the stylist and said, 'Give me the Emma look,'" Sara Bruna Quiñónez Estrada, Sinaloa's then attorney general and, before that, a feared judge, told me on a visit to her office one day in February 2022. "And it made me wonder how we have gotten to this point, that this woman is a prototype for others of all social classes."[4]

The aesthetic is known as the *buchona* look, a local term used to refer to women who are romantically or sexually involved with narcos. Some women traffickers and killers have epitomized the look, most recently Claudia Ochoa Félix, who was one of the original buchonas—the girlfriend of a prominent trafficker and a woman who reportedly grew into a violent and powerful killer for the Sinaloa Cartel in her own right. She, like Emma, understood the value of social media in building a brand, and her accounts on Instagram and Twitter pictured her buchona persona, posing with guns, yachts, and expensive cars. Hers was a more aggressive image than Emma's, even as she denied rumors that she was a cartel killer. Ochoa Félix died in 2019, reportedly of a drug overdose, in her home in Culiacán, but her legend lives on in a number of social media accounts. Inspiration, perhaps, for the current social media generation.

The buchona look isn't just the prereserve of those in the drug business. The woman I described at the beginning of this chapter, who pulled the trigger on the shooting range that day under the hot Sinaloan sun, looks strikingly like Emma. But her name is Tessa, and she is an accountant and a mother of two with nothing to do with the drug trade other than having grown up around it.

The buchona figure cannot be attained through unlimited hours in the gym. The exaggerated bust and rump in proportion to the tiny waist, the narrow nose, the full lips, the white skin—all of that comes at a price in Sinaloa's booming plastic surgery industry. Think Kim Kardashian meets Morticia Addams. Long, straight dark hair. The nails. Everything Gucci, Versace, or Prada.

"[Emma Coronel] is like an artist," Janet Martínez Quintero, thirty-eight, told me as we sat on a couple of sofas in an exclusive hair salon and yoga studio in central Culiacán in February 2021. "On top of all that, she's also one of the most beautiful women from here."[5]

Martínez Quintero didn't look a day over thirty, with clear white skin and blonde hair. Her cheekbones were perfectly high, her nose perfectly narrow and straight. She had her first plastic surgery operation when she was eighteen years old, she told me. A liposculpting was her first treatment, during which the surgeon removes excess fat from the waist, upper arms and back, and sculpts the glutes. Since then, she has had more than a dozen other treatments, including implants in her breasts and calves, and the removal of fat from inside her cheeks. It's a family tradition, she told me. Her mother and four sisters have also had plenty of surgery. Her nineteen-year-old son had just gifted a boob job to his girlfriend.

"Here, it is in our roots, all of us," she explained. "So in your country, where you live, they use one thing; in other countries they don't. Each country has its culture, right? And here what the older sister does, the youngest sister does, afterwards her daughter follows, and it goes on like that. I mean, it's something that is very established. . . . What the elders do, we want to do too. Like what the mother does, the daughter does, the granddaughter—it's a chain like that."

It was a tough interview, during which I felt deeply conflicted. A goal in my work is to try to leave judgment at the door. To do my best to fully immerse myself as much as possible in the life and story of the person in front of me—be they a victim, a killer, a friend, or a fiend. I have always reached for the empathy that is essential to truly understand the experience of another person. Talking with Janet, I realized that were I to look at a photo of her as a teenager, I would see very little left of that young woman in the person in front of me now. Nearly every single part of her had been nipped and tucked and tweaked, made smaller, bigger, smoother, or whiter. She had had surgeries and treatments that I hadn't even known existed.

"Surgery is something that satisfies you, that fills you up, that you like," she said. What she was saying went hard against so much of what I had been working for all my life. Self-acceptance. Love for the parts of me I didn't like but couldn't change. And hard work to improve those parts of me that I could change, both physical and emotional. But she saw it differently. Ultimately, my analysis of her probably does come from a personal judgment, which is uncomfortable for me to admit.

"When you get surgery, it's like a gift from God, that if there's something you don't like about yourself and you have the ability and the money to change it, you can. It raises your self-esteem," said Janet. "That's how the culture works here. If a woman doesn't like her body, and she has the opportunity to ask a man or a boyfriend, whatever, then they gift her that. They go and they pay for it with pleasure."

Another woman in the salon had traveled from California for lipo and a boob job. She told me that the attraction of having surgery in Mexico is that it's a better value for the money, but also that the doctors here are prepared to go further than they will elsewhere. "Here, like, I don't know, it just feels like, it's not that they're going against guidelines. . . . Just the way they mold your body, I feel like they just do a better job," she said.⁶

There are so many ways in which women may not like their bodies, and for women like Janet, surgery is the answer. Not eating well, not working out, not therapy. It did make sense to me. There is always more than one way to get to the same destination. But from my perspective, the cost-benefit ratio did seem to vary. I could see, for example, how nipping and tucking could get addictive. Much of what we don't like about ourselves has as much to do with our emotional and psychological makeup, lived experiences, emotional conditioning, and trauma, as it does with what we actually see in the mirror. Janet acknowledged that using surgery to mend those dissatisfactions was addictive. What she didn't address was the possibility that adjusting the physical is unlikely to get to the root of what is an emotional issue.

"One thing leads to another," said Janet. "I get my bum done, and then I look at my breasts and say, I'll get those done. And then after that you notice that your nose is slightly off, or you sharpen your chin. Then you think maybe a bit of Botox on the eyes will look even better, and higher cheekbones would help too. No? Then you get your legs done, you get calf implants. And one thing leads to another because the moment you have surgery you get addicted to it."

Being hooked on self-improvement of the surgical kind could be just another version of the constant search for growth and self-improvement. It isn't my version, but it did seem to be Janet's, and I respect that. My sense was that she considered my boyish, athletic figure and small post-baby breasts something I didn't have to suffer with unless I chose to. She may have even found my predicament unsettling or confusing. If I could afford to pump up my boobs and get the odd nip and tuck after having kids, then why on earth wouldn't I?

I can't say it has never crossed my mind to use surgery to improve the parts of me I don't love, but something always stops me: Not wanting to go under the knife again after two C-sections and a hernia operation. Not wanting to give in to my vanity. Fear of the outcome should things not turn out as desired. None of these sentiments come from good places, and all bring judgment to the decision to self-improve under the knife. I guess I'm not as nonjudgmental as I would like to be.

I started the interview aware of a persistent belief that buchonas are often forced by their narco boyfriends to have plastic surgery. I am sure it has happened, but the idea that the buchona look was imposed on Janet by her husband or the narco patriarchy is too simplistic an explanation of her desires and those of many women in Sinaloa. As many said to me during my research in Culiacán, women compete with each other as they strive for "beauty," in the same way they do for the attention of men. Now, perhaps they're aspiring to ideals that are defined by men. But as many residents of Sinaloa told me, if a narco man pushes his wife to make herself more attractive and noticeable, it can become a problem, as it attracts competition, i.e., other men.

To see women as one-dimensional victims in this body-sculpting trend is to oversimplify the matter. Having grown up around the culture of surgery, Janet simply doesn't seem to question the underlying values and dynamics behind it. In the same way that I might not question the wisdom of using exercise, diet, or therapy to improve my physical health, appearance, and mental wellbeing. For her, it is what it is, no questions asked. But people who grow up immersed in the same culture can still behave differently. Not all women in Sinaloa, or Mexico, subscribe to the dictated aesthetics of las buchonas.

The adherence to buchona standards contributes to what can be described as an increasing commodification of the female body. Plastic surgery, according to one well-respected female surgeon I interviewed, and as Janet suggested, is generally paid for by the women's male partners, and from the surgeon's perspective, seems to be another form of control. It was as much about the provision of the surgery and everything that it brought for women as the aesthetic that it produced. Because if your husband or boyfriend paid for your tits and ass, rightly or wrongly, it gives him a sense of ownership over you. Which makes it easier for him to treat you as a possession, and even dispose of you, should the need arise. And the aesthetic here stands apart from the love of plastic surgery in other parts of the world, because in other parts of the world, men don't routinely kill and dismember their women, or the women of other men, to send a message, the way they do in Sinaloa and in the drug trade generally. Special types of violence are reserved for women in these spaces. To make a point.

"If women live in those circumstances, in which men are the providers and give them luxuries and everything else, they pay for it later," María Teresa Guerra Ochoa, head of Sinaloa's state women's ministry, told me in her government office one morning. "If the women ever want to leave the relationship and live alone and in freedom, well, they often end up being killed. There are many stories like that."[7]

I wanted to know if I was misreading the situation, so I sought out Doctor Rafaela Martínez Terrazas, Janet's lifelong plastic surgeon. Sitting in the waiting room of her clinic, I was surrounded by women, each with some part of her body in bandages or plaster. They were all very young. A telenovela played on low volume on a TV, in which the female protagonists looked disconcertingly like the women who sat around me in the waiting room.

Dr. Martínez Terrazas has spent much of her career perfecting the Emma, or buchona, look. She is considered one of Culiacán's best plastic surgeons, attracting clients from the US and other parts of the world. It took me a while to get her to sit down for an interview with me, but once I had managed to lock her in and had waited an hour in her waiting room, I was richly rewarded. "I've always thought that men dominate women in three ways," she told me, as we sat in her office just off of the room where her operating table lay. "With their fists, with money, and via their self-esteem. Their men don't want them to become empowered."[8]

A basic lipo procedure, which removes fat from the upper arms, thighs, and stomach, brings in the waistline, and pumps up the *pompis* (butt cheeks), costs around $5,000. While some of these women have their procedures paid for by their husbands or boyfriends, these men are calculated about the payment process. "They don't hand women the cash, because when women get money, if they're smart, they start to save or empower themselves a little through economic independence. And their men are never going to allow that to happen," said Dr. Martínez Terrazas, shaking her head. She is discreet about the men and women she has operated on over the last few decades, but she is also fully aware that many of them are involved in the drug trade. "But women like depending on their men . . . that they have to ask them for money for everything, even a kilo of tortillas."

Again, the issue of agency arose as I listened to what she told me. These women feel that life doesn't include a wide range of options, and they make their choices accordingly. That more options may be available is not the point. The options that women perceive are the only ones that count. For many women immersed in narco culture, the idea of tooling up to get a job to gain financial independence might not be in that range of what seems possible. Latin American women are often not encouraged by those around them to question the traditional values and lifestyles that have been passed on through generations. Instead, they make decisions within the parameters their cultural context dictates. That includes the tradition of finding a man who can take care of them and provide everything they want and need.

"Mexico hasn't yet managed to construct enough opportunities for the economic empowerment of women," said Guerra Ochoa. "So the route to drug trafficking has become the shortest road to riches, and humans in general tend to choose the easiest route to success. So many women take that road."

The point isn't to *be* a narco or a buchona but to look like one. "For many Sinaloan women, their life's focus is to marry a narco because of what it implies—the lifestyle, clothes, house, cars," Isaac Tomás Guevara Martínez, a social psychologist who studies violence in the state of Sinaloa, told me on a reporting trip. "Emma Coronel is the prototype of the ideal body type for many women."[9]

But in Culiacán's plastic surgery culture, things can go horribly wrong. In early 2022, news broke about a young woman, Paulina Ramírez García, age twenty-six, who desperately wanted to look like Emma Coronel. But after getting the lipo, Paulina developed an infection. Further examination revealed that her internal organs had been damaged during the procedure, and she died on March 9, 2022 after three difficult weeks in hospital.[10] "It's common that there are pseudo-surgeons who 'operate,' and this isn't the first victim of this 'doctor' and others," Dr. Martínez Terrazas said about Paulina's case, which she thinks is "the tip of the iceberg."

There's no way of knowing how many women die like this.

The doctor who performed the procedure on Paulina—Dr. Amayrani Adilene Rodríguez Pérez—was not a qualified plastic surgeon but rather a general practitioner, according to the state prosecutor. She was operating in one of dozens of clandestine, unlicensed "clinics" that have popped up "exponentially" over the last two years across Sinaloa, according to Randy Ross, a commissioner from the local public health risk-prevention agency, Comisión Estatal para la Protección contra Riesgos Sanitarios, known by its Spanish acronym, Coepris. Six months after Ramírez García's death, Coepris inspectors closed twenty-four such clinics for failing to meet the basic requirements. But the vast majority of the clinics like the one that allegedly killed Paulina don't even register with the authorities and operate completely under the radar.[11]

I went to the place where Paulina got her surgery: a plain, white building on the side of a road on the outskirts of Culiacán that was utterly inconspicuous. There were no visual signs of what went on behind those doors, which Ross says is a common characteristic of these sorts of clandestine clinics.

Social media has amplified the buchona subculture, and it is no longer just the reserve of the state's narco-royalty. Type Emma Coronel, or the word "buchona," into the Instagram search box, and dozens of accounts appear showing women with impossible bodies and Facebook is littered with surgery providers, both real and fake.

The adulation of narcocultura poses other risks to women, aside from the narco-sanctioned "look." Claudia Ochoa Félix, perhaps the most famous female *sicario*, or hired killer, connected to the Sinaloa

Cartel, was widely adored in the culture, as is Melissa "La China" Calderon. La China was arrested in 2015 and is now serving life in a Mexican prison for allegedly killing some 150 people on behalf of Dámaso López, the former right-hand man of El Chapo. When I asked for an interview, the Mexican government told me she refused the request from her cell. There's no way to be certain that is the truth. A profile of her in the *Daily Beast* explains how "La China led an army of murderers, then went rogue, terrorizing Cabo San Lucas with a fleet of 300 killers. She might have kept at it—if her lover hadn't snitched."[12]

The younger generations in Sinaloa, especially, idolize such women. Fifteen-year-old Yazmín Esmeralda, while visiting her grandmother in Guasave, in northwestern Sinaloa, discovered an Uzi submachine gun at the bottom of a closet. She felt inspired to use it to pose for the "best TikTok video of her life," according to reports in the local press. She was posing for the camera held by her younger brother when the gun went off, killing her instantly. Her mother told reporters that she found Yazmín facedown in a pool of her own blood.[13]

So many questions went off in my head when I read about Yazmín's death: What was an Uzi doing in her grandmother's house, and why was it left within reach of children? Why would she want to be seen posing with a gun like that?

"Narco culture is aspirational," said Siria Gastélum, who was born and raised in Culiacán. She has studied mafias for most of her professional life and works for the Global Initiative Against Transnational Organized Crime (GITOC). "Way before social media existed, we had *narcocorridos*. It was all about showing off, being a legend. Youth is always shopping for heroes, rockstars, and role models."[14]

"That [Yazmín] chose to record a clip [in that way] shows that our youth is immersed in that culture," said Sara Bruna Quiñónez Estrada, Sinaloa's attorney general. "It's what they hear about at all hours."[15]

The universality of these ideals and aspirations doesn't make tragedies like those of Paulina and Yazmín any easier to stomach.

"THEM"

When the miniature plaster version of El Chapo first appeared in the Malverde chapel back in 2019, it cost around 750 pesos (around $37). But on a trip back a few years later for this book in February 2022, I found that the cost of the statue had doubled. The woman behind the stall at the chapel who sold one to me said that not just anyone can make the mini-Chapos. Producers have to have permission. From "them," she said.

She probably meant Iván Archivaldo Guzmán Salazar, Ovidio Guzmán López, and Jesús Alfredo Guzmán Salazar—Chapo's adult sons, collectively known as Los Chapitos, or the Mini Chapos, who are the new bosses in Culiacán. Following Chapo's extradition, they went to war with their father's former right-hand man, Dámaso López, in a bloody struggle for control of parts of Sinaloa and its lucrative drug cultivation plots, as well as its meth and fentanyl labs. Then there was Ismael "El Mayo" Zambada, one of the last remaining old-school drug legends, who displayed little loyalty to Chapo's boys as they used new levels of violence to try and establish their rule. "[Los Chapitos] command fear. Not respect. That's a big difference [from the old generation]," one resident of Culiacán told me.[16]

Emma Coronel knows how the men of Sinaloa tick. She grew up around them. She knows that, for them, business is business. Following Chapo's sentencing to life in prison in July 2019, she felt that no one—not his grown adult sons, not his former lifelong business partner El Mayo, nor anyone else left in his close circle—would let her history with Chapo get in the way if it was going to obstruct their business interests. She knew that they were thinking about what she knew and what she might be able to offer US prosecutors in the way of building cases against those left in the game.

Those fears were exacerbated by the violence that exploded across the state when Chapo was taken out of the country. Emma was wary about getting caught in the crossfire, which is why she wanted to learn to shoot a gun, among other self-defense techniques, to protect herself. She frequently took a practical approach to her position and predicament.

El Chapo's lover, Lucero Sanchez, told a court in New York in January 2019 how she and Chapo were awakened while together one night by a police raid in Culiacán in 2014. The lovers had to run naked through sewer tunnels to escape. Emma, who was sitting in the courtroom as Lucero gave her testimony, is reported to have cackled with laughter as her husband's former lover broke down in tears.

"Coronel's glee was only exacerbated when Sanchez's lapel mic remained on even after she was removed for a break—her sobs still being broadcast throughout the courtroom after she left," wrote the *New York Post*'s Emily Saul and Ruth Brown.[17] My guess is that trying to prevent or ignore the fact that her husband took lovers was futile and a waste of emotional energy, so instead Emma made light of it.

"I am not so sure that Emma really loved Chapo Guzmán," Mike Vigil, a former chief of DEA international operations in Mexico, told me. "They knew each other for such a short period of time before they got married. With him on the lam, she had access to all of his money, and she was able to lead a very affluent life, if you will, and not have to deal with Chapo that much."[18]

By the time Emma and Chapo met and married, he was a famous fugitive. It's unlikely that she and the drug lord ever shared a home like a typical married couple, and she would have been under constant surveillance by both Mexican and American agents on the chance that she might lead them to her husband. It's unlikely that Chapo—who spent most of his time hiding in the mountains of Sinaloa and other remote parts of the region—was sitting around twiddling his thumbs or gazing longingly into the distance in between doodling pictures of Emma.

"He had a ton of mistresses," Vigil told me.

"Many women [who marry narcos]—like the young women who marry some old hedge fund guy because they want the life he can provide—settle," Bonnie Klapper, a criminal lawyer in the US who has represented a number of female drug traffickers, told me. "They understand their lives won't be normal ones. But either they don't want to leave because they like their lives, or they are afraid to leave because they know the narco husband will come after them."[19]

Who knows whether Emma followed the same policy as her husband regarding fidelity, but she definitely understood his deal. The marriage was a partnership, one arguably more of business than pleasure. Little evidence exists that there was an emotional connection between them, which suggests that she did not take his womanizing at all seriously.

What she did take seriously was her security and that of her twin daughters. Learning how to handle a gun proved unable to protect her from what was to come, and in February 2021, less than two years after her husband had been convicted and was subsequently sentenced to life in a US prison, she was taken into custody as well. When she landed in Washington, DC, she was detained on drug trafficking charges and accusations that she had helped Chapo with his second maximum-security jailbreak in July 2015. He had slipped out of his cell via a hole in the floor of his shower stall and then gotten on a motorbike mounted on rails and sped to freedom through a specially constructed well-lit ventilated tunnel.

It later emerged that Emma had turned herself in.[20] She was eventually sentenced to just three years behind bars—a very short sentence given the charges against her—which fueled speculation that she had cooperated on other cases related to her husband. Given these circumstances, it's unlikely, following her release, that she will ever return to Sinaloa looking for the vestiges of her old life.

THE ETERNAL SEARCH

A silent crowd of women watch as the claw of the excavator makes easy work of the sand. The hole that the machine is gouging into the ground grows deeper and wider. The pile of sand that the claw dumps to the side grows higher, and, eventually, two women pick up a giant sieve and start loading it with sand from the massive mound and sifting it as though looking for gold. And they are looking for a treasure of sorts. Teeth, bones, buttons, hair clips, clothes, earrings, or anything else that remains of their missing loved ones. What might be left of their sons, daughters, husbands, sisters, brothers.

A small sand-covered lump tumbles into view as the claw pulls away from the hole. The silence deepens. One of the women uses a shovel to pull it out. It is a small part of vertebrae. "*Donde estan? Donde estan?* [Where are they? Where are they?]" some of the women start to chant, as though in a religious ceremony. The bone fragment is placed to the side of the hole. Photos are taken. Phone calls are made.

A man who used to work for a drug cartel rang María Isabel Cruz Bernal, founder of the collective *Las Sabuesas* (loosely, "bloodhounds" or "sleuths") a few days before my visit in February 2022. He was repentant about some of the dirty work that he had done for his bosses: killing, dismembering, and burying. He thought that María and her fellow women might be able to find something—someone—buried in the sands of El Pozo, a known dumping ground and conflict zone for local criminal groups.

Las Sabuesas is composed mostly of women who are looking for their missing children or other relatives. María's son Yosimar, who was a police officer, was abducted from their family home in January 2017 by a group of armed men. He hasn't been seen since. "Yosimar won't appear, *el cabrón* [bastard]," said María. She hasn't found a single sign of him since her search began more than five years ago.[21] As she and I spoke, the other women loaded shovels and iron poles into the back of a truck. They use the poles to stick deep into the ground where they think that bodies might be buried, then pull them out and smell the ends for the putrid stench of decay. The truck that carried the women and their shovels and sticks to different sites belongs to a government search commission. The State Commission for Missing People was providing the excavator machine.

Dozens of groups like this set off on similar searches across Mexico every week, searching for more than one hundred thousand people who have gone missing in the last two decades, many of them since the country's "drug war" began in 2007.[22] More than twenty-one thousand have gone missing since President Andrés Manuel López Obrador (referred to by his initials, AMLO, in Mexico) took power in 2018.[23] The members of these groups are, without doubt, doing the government's dirty work, despite promises during AMLO's campaign that he would resolve Mexico's missing persons crisis. That has not transpired.

Officials often excuse their lack of action in this area by dismissing the victims as henchmen or lookouts for organized crime. Once someone goes missing, the victimization can deepen. Mothers can spend years looking for closure—a body to bury. Until then, they don't consider themselves in mourning.

"What was your son's name?" I asked Mirtha Mendoza the day following the search, while sitting in the front room of her small house in a middle-class suburb of Culiacán.

"His name *is* José Manuel Macías Alfonso," she corrected me softly. "Because for me, he is not dead. So that's why I say he *is called*, not *was*." On the afternoon of November 12, 2017, José Manuel, age twenty-nine, whom everyone called "Junior," was on his way with his girlfriend to eat lunch with his mother when their Uber was stopped by a white Suburban truck, Mirtha told me. A number of armed men got out, ordered him out of his car, bundled him into theirs, and took him away. Shocked and terrified, his girlfriend rushed to Mirtha's house and told her what had happened.[24]

"I was completely consumed by fear," Mirtha remembered. "When I heard his girlfriend talk about armed men, I was convinced that they were coming for us." Four or five days went by before Mirtha went to see a young man in the neighborhood whom she asked for help looking for Junior. She didn't specify to me who this young man was or what he did. He made a phone call. "Yes, they have your son," he told her. "He's very beaten up." Mirtha begged him to beg them to let him go. To tell them that she didn't want any trouble. That she just wanted him back. But they didn't give him back, and four years later, Mirtha is a regular on the Sabuesas outings like the one in El Pozo.

I have spent days with these sorts of groups during my fifteen years in Mexico, and in states other than Sinaloa. Officially, there are some five thousand people reported missing in Sinaloa. María, the Sabuesas founder, thinks that the real number is twice that, and that her group alone has found more than sixteen thousand pieces of "treasure," human remains, since they started looking. Since the drug war began, Mexico's forensics services have been inundated by corpses. It is a sobering and stomach-churning truth. At the time of writing this book, the AMLO administration recommended the creation of a special Center for Human Identification, in the hope of matching many of the unidentified bodies festering in the country's morgues with the grief-stricken families and loved ones looking for them.

During the interview with Mirtha in her house, her husband arrives. He grunts a hello, and then disappears into one of the back bedrooms. He doesn't want to talk to me, and he doesn't want to talk about Junior. It is a pattern I've seen a lot around this topic—it is more often than not the women who are the driving force behind trying to find missing people. Mirtha says that her search for Junior is an extension of her domestic duties. That her husband goes to work and earns money, while looking for her son is just another part of her childcare responsibilities.

But María says it goes deeper than that. "I think [the women do it because] our insides are clamoring for the part of us that was stolen. I think us mothers are missing a part of our insides."

I am struggling to find the words to describe what it might feel like to dig in the dirt for the remains of the baby you gave birth to. The prospect leaves me mute. I prefer numbness to feeling even a fraction of that horror. I find myself turning away from the effort to empathize with these women because of fear, terror, an incapacity to conceive of that ever being a reality. These women are the embodiment of resilience. This is living in some of the most severe daily discomfort, pain, and uncertainty that life can bring. These women, and thousands of others, get out of bed to do this every single day all over the country. However old their children were when they went missing, and whatever some of them might have been tied up in before they disappeared, for mothers like María and Mirtha and their *compañeras* (colleagues), there is no other option but to search until they find them.

And yet, even at such depths of darkness, something gorgeous takes shape that day in El Pozo. After a few hours of following the government workers around in their excavator, the women take a break. Lupita Valdez, whose son was also taken by armed men, in July 2018, lays down a blanket. The women around her pull out an array of plastic boxes from their backpacks containing *tinga* (shredded chicken in tomato sauce), *frijoles* (beans), white cheese, and other fillings. Supermarket *tortillas* wrapped in crackling paper appear, as well as a few bottles of Coca-Cola. I watch them from a few meters away as I shelter under a tree to try to escape the relentless afternoon sun and bat away the tiny flies that are everywhere. The women gesture to me to eat, but I feel like an intruder all of a sudden. I don't want to interrupt their brief relief, their reverie. They remove their facemasks, which they are wearing both because of COVID and the dirt that the search stirs up. Lupita makes a joke, and the rest of the women burst out laughing.

"I can't imagine my life without the Sabuesas collective," Mirtha tells me from her sofa at home, where she says she slept for the first two years after Junior was taken, hoping to hear his footsteps on the front porch. Now, she sleeps in her bed. "I have so much to thank María [Cruz, the Sabuesas founder] for. If it wasn't for them, I do not know who I would be today."

Unless you are one, being around grieving mothers is hard, a contact of mine said to me when we were talking about the Sabuesas collectives. But groups such as these bring women suffering the same pain together, and they give María, Mirtha, Lupita, and thousands of others not only hope and activity but companionship in a journey that may well last the rest of their lives.

RESISTANCE

On that Sunday morning in the already searing sun, when Tessa and I pick up guns for the first time, we and the other two women in the class are under the tuition of Abel Jacobo Miller. The demand from women to learn how to manage weapons and their own bodies under pressure has surged in recent years, Jacobo Miller told me during the few days that I spent with him. He is hell-bent on trying to convince many ordinary women in Culiacán to learn self-defense. "You have to learn not to rely on anyone—not your boyfriend, not your husband—to defend you. You have to learn how to defend yourself," Jacobo Miller tells the class. He has a gun in his hand, but he points to his head and says, "This is your most important weapon."[25]

Across town from the shooting range the day before, more women gathered in a gym on the outskirts of the city to learn basic self-defense techniques. After the course, which showed them how to react to physical attacks, I spoke to some of the women there. Many of them had suffered heinous gender violence. Maria López told me that she was kidnapped in a restaurant in broad daylight by a group of young cartel henchmen. She was held captive for four days, along with some friends of hers. During that time, she said she was raped repeatedly. "And not just by one of them," she says. "By all of them."[26] After the first few days in captivity, she said, she started asking the men what they wanted sexually, and how, so that they'd stop beating her when they raped her. "You have to go with the flow to survive," she said.

Kathleen, a slight blonde woman with blue eyes and arms peppered with tattoos, said she was attacked by her boyfriend six months earlier when she was at his house with him and his parents. "He stormed into the bathroom and got me into a stranglehold. I was so shocked, I could only put my hand on his hand—I was suffocating," she said. He let her go, and she fell to the floor, where he proceeded to kick her in the ribs until his parents rushed in to intervene. Her own family subsequently blamed her for the attack, accusing her of asking for trouble by being at her boyfriend's house at that time of night.[27]

Jacobo Miller demonstrated for the women how to get out of a stranglehold, and he shouted, "You can't think that you're not going to stab your husband! He's strangling you! He's trying to kill you!" He and his wife, Ana, who have three daughters, are determined to change the mindset of the women of Culiacán. Ana will never forget the afternoon now widely known as Black Thursday, when she was stuck in traffic with her three daughters. "Suddenly I saw people getting out of their cars, grabbing their children, and running away," she recalled. Then a young man standing on the edge of the road, wearing a black mask, started firing a Barrett rifle into the air. "I was hysterical with fear," she remembered.[28]

———

That day—October 17, 2019—a war broke out between the government and cartel henchmen in the heart of Culiacán, after army officers attempted to arrest one of El Chapo's older sons, Ovidio. The episode was a clear indication of who governed the city and a humiliation for the administration of President López Obrador.

The struggle for control of Sinaloa is unlikely to ever end. New generations will continue to kill each other for the spoils of the drug trade. Emma Coronel has left the stage for now, while Chapo's sons, roughly the same age as she is, are vying to control the cartel their father left behind. The women I have met during my many trips to Sinaloa will, I know, continue to live in the conditions the drug culture dictates.

But although Emma, even in prison in the US, is perhaps the most visible woman of the Sinaloa Cartel, she is far from the most powerful.

CHAPTER 7

THE FEMALE CHAPO

The city of Hermosillo sits in the middle of the baking desert in the Northern Mexican state of Sonora. Mesquite trees line its scorched highways, which are littered with the charred bodies of the bold rattlesnakes who dare to cross the asphalt in the searing sun.

Two brothers with the surname Avilés Fajardo were driving on one of those highways in late April 2017, most likely on their way to their mother's local methamphetamine laboratory. The men, along with their sister Arlene, managed the lab as part of the family drug trafficking business, which was based to the south across the state line in Sinaloa.

The brothers, who might have had their mother's large brown eyes, dark hair, and good looks, were stopped by someone on that highway that day. Probably more than one person. Whoever made them pull up onto the side of the road likely used the persuasive powers of high-caliber weapons. The identity of the aggressors remains unknown, but their mother, Luz Irene Fajardo Campos, has her suspicions about the motive for what came next, and who was behind it.

After the brothers were stopped, or "kidnapped" according to court documents, they were ordered out of their vehicle. Then they were tortured. It's possible that the torture did not take place on the side of a highway for passersby to see. The details of the abuse aren't publicly known. Perhaps we do not need to know. Those facts might be too much for their mother, who has already had to bear the loss of two of her children.

After they were tortured, the brothers were returned to their truck on the side of the highway. Then their bodies were set on fire while they were still alive. But the aggressors didn't leave it at that. By the time their burned bodies were found, they had no heads, which, of course, made it harder for them to be identified.[1]

————

The boys' mother, Luz, was once described in court as the female equivalent of Joaquín "El Chapo" Guzmán. As the "female face" of the Sinaloa Cartel.[2] When Luz's sons were pulled over on that sun-scorched highway, prosecutors to the north in the US were preparing for the start of the New York trial of El Chapo, perhaps the most important organized crime case of a generation.

Yet, despite El Chapo's arrest, business continued to boom for the Sinaloa Cartel, and Luz and her family organization carried on trafficking drugs and enjoying the spoils, thanks to their "close affiliation" with Chapo's organization, according to a former associate of hers. Prior to Guzmán's arrest, the two would regularly speak by phone, allegedly. Unbeknownst to them, investigators had tapped Luz's phones and messages dating back to 2013. However, none of her supposed conversations with Chapo were ever used as evidence against her.

Luz's case is nuanced, and a complex woman emerges from the limited information provided by her case. She was an independent woman who, the evidence suggests, was running an illicit business with the help of her sons. But unlike Chapo's organization, hers did so without the violent terror tactics. During her years in the trade, Luz was a successful and powerful patrona who also seemed warm-hearted and personable, often sharing family photos with her business associates.

Following the murder of her sons, Luz was subsequently handed down a heavy sentence—by the government that she blames for their deaths.[3]

————————

Days before her boys were killed, Luz, fifty-three at the time, was in Colombia. She later told a courtroom she was sent there to take "pictures of some people" for an associate of hers. Luz recalled that she was there only for a few days and had some meetings before it was time to head home. But on that day in early April, her driver kept "getting lost," causing her to miss her flight to Mexico from the capital, Bogotá. That was when she started to suspect that things might not go her way.[4]

When she finally got to the airport, Luz was stopped at immigration before she could board her plane. She recalled that she started to get nervous, and her stomach began to ache and twist. She rushed to the bathroom and threw up. After waiting for a few hours, she was led into a room to meet with a Colombian prosecutor. Luz told the prosecutor that she needed to speak to someone from the DEA, which he agreed with. "You have to get out [of Colombia] . . . as soon as you can. Negotiate with the DEA," he said. He seemed to be trying to help her, but Luz wasn't sure.

She wouldn't get out any time soon. For the next few months, Luz was kept in Colombian custody and sat through hours of meetings. "There were approximately thirty-seven hours of conversations with the prosecution during a period of about six or seven months, during which time I was never allowed to speak.," she recalled. "All the talking was done by the DEA agents. Always."

Luz had much to share with the agents, who by then had been reading the messages on the Blackberry she had used to conduct her drug trafficking operation out of Mexico for years. But her main concern during those meetings wasn't her possible incarceration. It was her family's safety. "I begged and I warned them about the danger involved in this," she told Judge John D. Bates before her sentencing hearing in Washington, DC, years later. As far as Luz is concerned, it was her detention and those subsequent meetings behind closed doors in Bogotá that led to the murder of her two boys.

It's Luz's belief that her arrest and much of her conversation with the DEA agents when she was first detained in Colombia were leaked to criminal associates and rivals in Mexico. They then went after her sons to shut her business down, as well as to shut her up and discourage her from cooperating with US prosecutors. By then, the reins of the Sinaloa Cartel were in the hands of other leaders following the conviction of El Chapo, most significantly those of Chapo's four sons, known collectively as Los Chapitos. They have a reputation for being hyper-violent and entitled millennials. People fear them, but they don't respect them the way they did their father.

Luz knew her sons were at risk as soon as she was detained, but her pleas to the DEA to take precautions went unaddressed. "I think if you asked her about what America does to people in jail and to foreign nationals that are extradited," her lawyer, Robert Feitel, told the judge, "she would say it kills their children."[5]

————

Family mattered to Luz. She was born and raised near the tiny picturesque town of Cosalá, Sinaloa, which is home to some seven thousand people. Here, generations of families pass down property and land to each other. Everyone knows everyone. She was one of many siblings growing up in a community long surrounded by drug plant cultivation. Cosalá lies in a part of Mexico known as the Golden Triangle, where heroin poppy and weed have been cultivated in clandestine plots in the mountains by humble farming communities for decades. Luz knew and understood the drug trade and how the Sinaloa Cartel was a de facto parallel power to the government in Sinaloa, as well as a buyer of heroin poppy paste and marijuana from swaths of farmers.

Accounts of Luz's early years are mixed. She has a law degree, which requires a university education and suggests hopes to practice law professionally. No doubt, Luz probably had to leave the tiny towns around Cosalá for at least Culiacán, if not the capital of Mexico City, to study. But her life before that wasn't easy. Rural communities in Mexico are very often made up of big families living in grinding poverty. Alcohol abuse and domestic violence are common. According to court documents, she was raised by her maternal grandparents and grew up "poor." It's unclear why she wasn't raised by her mother and father. I wondered whether she felt some sense of abandonment because she was left with her grandparents.

By the time she was a teenager, Luz was becoming well-acquainted with the rural macho culture around her. She was abducted and raped by a group of men before she was eighteen, according to reports submitted to the court during her trial. There are no further details about that incident, but the experience was "certainly a very meaningful and horrific event," Judge Bates said prior to her sentencing, noting that it had a detrimental effect on her mental health from an early age.

Things didn't get much better after that. Around the time she was attacked, her grandparents brokered a forced marriage for their granddaughter with a man who "physically and sexually abused her and later did apparently something even more with one of their children before the defendant ultimately left him and was on her own with her children."[6]

Those two experiences at such a young age likely had a profound impact on Luz's view of the world and the men around her. Even the judge said that both incidents could have ultimately pushed her into the drug trade, especially after leaving her abusive husband and finding herself alone with mouths to feed. It's not clear how many children she has, but there are at least four, including the three sons and daughter who worked with her.

By the time she was called to support her family alone, Luz was acutely aware of her vulnerabilities as a woman. I wonder whether the thought of being at the mercy of another powerful man in exchange for financial support just didn't appeal to her. All partnerships come with their costs, and marriage is no different. She probably didn't have the stomach for making any more sacrifices in that respect, and other than her children, there are no other male family members visible in the evidence used against her in court.

When Luz started trafficking around 2010, the only men she counted on intimately to do her business were her own sons, much like El Chapo with his boys. After the extradition of their father in 2017, a violent struggle for power erupted across Sinaloa between different factions of the Sinaloa Cartel, mostly famously between Los Chapitos (Chapo's sons Iván, Ovidio, Joaquín, and Jesús, who remain at large today) and Dámaso López, also known as "El Licenciado," their father's former confidant and right-hand man. López, a former prison chief, helped Chapo make his first great escape from a maximum-security prison in 2001. But after El Chapo was sent north, the relationship between López and Los Chapitos soured.

López allegedly tried to kill Iván and Jesús in an ambush on a Sinaloan highway in February 2017, weeks after their father's extradition. Both brothers were injured but survived the attack, and the ambush detonated a violent war between the two sides. López only survived because he was arrested and detained in Mexico City. The Mexican government, working in collaboration with US officials, did Los Chapitos a solid. López's extradition to the US in July 2018 assured them that he was out of the picture for good and shored up the brothers' control of Culiacán. Challenges will come and go, and the brothers continued to live in a fragile peace agreement with their father's former associate and Sinaloa Cartel cofounder Ismael "El Mayo" Zambada, as well as other rivals.

And it's not just their criminal competitors who are out for their blood.

On October 17, 2019, an attempt to arrest Ovidio in Culiacán by the Mexican government backfired horribly.[7] Ovidio was briefly taken into custody by the Mexican military, which prompted thousands of Sinaloa Cartel henchmen to take to the streets, creating a mini–civil war that played out across the city. Videos on social media show young men circling the streets on the back of trucks mounted with .50-caliber Barrett rifles, shooting at government troops on major streets in broad daylight. The government was forced to release Ovidio after government troops were outgunned and outnumbered in what proved to be a major embarrassment for the government of President Andrés Manuel López Obrador. Three years later, on January 5, 2023, Ovidio was again arrested and immediately flown to Mexico City and a high-security prison.

The other three sons who remain at large, now in their thirties and forties, each have a $5 million bounty on their heads, promised by the US government. Criminal cases against drug bosses like Los Chapitos are being built in the hope that they might be taken into custody someday, and collaborators like Luz can serve as key witnesses into how their criminal empires operate. This is probably why Luz's children were murdered. Killing them was a warning for her to keep her mouth shut. And whether that was the intended message or not, that is the message that she received.

Luz pleaded innocent, refused to cooperate, and went to trial. During any trial, the details of a case are made public, and there's no negotiating a lower sentence behind closed doors. But her move sent a clear message to her former criminal collaborators that she had kept her mouth shut. Today, her father, sister, and other family members continue to live in Sinaloa, where they could be targeted by the cartel as her sons were. "Who is going to see two of their kids kidnapped and murdered and then do anything to put the rest of their family at risk? Nobody is going to do that," Feitel, Luz's lawyer, told me.

Little happens in Culiacán without the knowledge of its criminal overlords. I'm sure that my investigations in the city did not go unnoticed. When I started looking into patronas of the Sinaloa Cartel, I spoke at length to a number of local journalists in the hope of understanding these women's personal lives and stories. After an initial conversation, none of them followed up or wanted anything else to do with my project. I get it—why put your head above the parapet?

No one in Mexico will ever forget the assassination of the country's most prominent narco-chronicler, Javier Valdez, who for years wrote about Sinaloa's drug trafficking landscape and TV-novelesque drama for the weekly newspaper, *Rio Doce*, that he helped found.

Valdez was the most prominent of dozens of journalists who have been slain in recent years across Mexico by both criminal and political powers.[8] Five years later, it was no wonder that other lesser-known reporters had no desire to delve into the criminal past of some of the Sinaloa Cartel's prominent operators, male or female. The kind of investigative work required to learn more about women, who are much more hidden than men within the ranks of organized crime, is highly dangerous for Mexican journalists. When I mentioned Luz and Guadalupe Fernández Valencia to many reporters, none of them had heard of either of them. They were completely unknown. I believe there are two reasons why these women are unheard of. The first is that investigating what is occurring in Sinaloa is extremely difficult. And the second is that there is a lack of interest in women drug traffickers within the journalistic community. As I continued my work in Sinaloa, much of my investigation into Luz's story was done alone.

Luz's father, Ignacio Fajardo Arroyo, was mentioned in the court documents of her case. In my research, I found that he was once a municipal president. I eventually tracked him down via social media, and after many errant phone calls and strange WhatsApp text message exchanges, he agreed to meet in Culiacán, Sinaloa, while I was researching there in May 2021. It was one of the strangest interviews that I've conducted in my career. In fact, to call it that feels somewhat inaccurate.

Ignacio, or Nacho as he is known locally, told me to meet him at a government agricultural building where he keeps a small office. Now in his eighties, he had a full head of hair that was gelled back onto his wide round head. Upon meeting me, he looked at me with suspicion through watery eyes. He came armed with a number of maps and legal documents, as though he had to argue a case, and spent the lion's share of our conversation telling me about a land dispute in which he was engaged near Cosalá, where, he claimed, someone was stealing his water. That our exchanges and my interview request via text up until that point had been exclusively about his daughter seemed to matter little, as did the fact that as we spoke, she was sitting in a jail cell in the US on drug trafficking charges.[9]

There was a general sense of discombobulation surrounding Nacho. But as I sat in front of him in that dated municipal government building on that hot Sinaloan afternoon, I knew I was probably as close as I would ever be to his daughter. I could see the physical similarity—wide-set eyes, thick skin, wide mouth. He confirmed the abduction and torture of her sons, and he told me that his daughter had earned her degree as a lawyer. I was surprised, because this meant Luz might have had other options than entering the drug trade. Nacho wasn't forthcoming about Luz's childhood. Probably because he hadn't been around much. And he certainly wasn't one of the few trusted men she had brought into her business.

———

She did, however, seem to have a fairly close relationship with El Chapo. But while Luz was referred to as the female Chapo in court proceedings, evidence suggests just how different her methods were from her male counterpart's.

In December 2014, an email landed in Rupert De Las Casas's inbox, offering him $100,000 for a week's work flying a Gulfstream III jet on an unspecified mission. The aging pilot was usually paid $1,500 a day working from his base in Florida, but he had hit hard times after getting fired from his job for his struggles with addiction. The offer, way above his usual pay rate and at a time when any work was looking unlikely, was tempting.

The email stated, "Our client is a very important person and want[s] full discretion NO Questions." This did not put him off. Nor did he believe that the offer of work involved anything legal. "Initially I thought we might be running guns or something like that, but after a while, when I realized we were going to Venezuela, I realized probably it was going to be running drugs," De Las Casas told a jury in Washington, DC, in December 2019, five years later.[10]

Which is how he found himself flying the Gulfstream airplane out of Mexico City, skirting Cancun, and heading south to Venezuela, an important cocaine transit hub. "Once we were clear of Mexican airspace, we turned off all our lights, all transponders, nearly all the lights in the cockpit too. Total—total silence," said De Las Casas.

It was Luz and her organization who had hired him to make that flight, prosecutors allege. It was her plane that he flew—one of an army of planes that she owned—and ultimately ruined in the Venezuelan jungle. The end of that black flight involved landing on a clandestine airstrip that wasn't equipped to take the weight of the jet, and by the time he grounded the plane in the darkness of the predawn morning, the left-hand side had sunk into the dirt, coming to a stop at a forty-five-degree angle. De Las Casas and his three-man crew turned off the engine and fled into the jungle, fearful of being discovered. Which the plane was, by the Venezuelan army. Shortly after they landed, the military flew over the wrecked Gulfstream III in their own military jets and blew it up, according to De Las Casas.

Essentially, the aging pilot made rather a mess of things. So did a guy called Mario Grado-Field. "Listen, you bastard," he told his brother Luis Carlos Torres over the phone from Tucson, Arizona, in August 2012. "I can't be going around with drugs like this."

"My boy, you're just going to deliver them," Torres tried to placate him from Mexico. Torres, who was also working for Luz, had sent the drugs to Grado-Field without any agreement between the two of them, Grado-Field claimed during his testimony during Luz's trial. When he was handed over a grocery bag in a car wash in Tucson, he found a bunch of methamphetamines inside. He was Mexican and had been living in the US for some thirty years by that point and had children and grandchildren living there. He didn't want any trouble, he claimed.

But he agreed to deliver the meth a few weeks later, which is when he got busted by the DEA. Then he lied to his brother back in Mexico and told him that he had dumped the car and fled when he got scared, and that the car had been reported stolen. He claimed the drugs were stolen before he could get the car back. In effect, Grado-Field had decided to cooperate with the DEA and was trying to keep both sides happy.

"I am going to give the lady [Luz] your telephone number so she can call you. You explain it to her," Torres said to Grado-Field about the lost drugs.

But when Luz spoke to both men about the fiasco, she did not threaten them with violence. Transcripts of those conversations show a calm, collected businesswoman. And that is the rub for me in this case: How did she manage to move so much blow *without* having to send in the heavies? The kind of heavies who killed her sons. The kind of heavies who delivered the message that a woman in this business needed to be taken seriously. But she knew how things worked—she never went anywhere without her bodyguard.

It's possible that Luz outsourced her muscle requirements to the Sinaloa Cartel. One former criminal associate told the DEA that at one point, when he was with Luz, she called El Chapo for a chat and then passed the phone over to him. "According to you, Ms. Fajardo was sort of the face—the female face of the Sinaloa Cartel, is that about right, according to your testimony?" Feitel, Luz's lawyer, asked the witness, Juan Erbe Favela, in court.[11]

"She was," he replied. "She had [Chapo] on the phone, and she passed the called phone on to me. She told me he was on the phone."

Having direct access to the *jefe de los jefes* is a privilege of only a high-ranking trafficker. It's possible that Luz was so close to the boss that she rang him directly when things got tough. But there is no further mention of El Chapo in her case files. The witness who made the statement—Erbe Favela—worked as a DEA informant for a total of nine years and was compensated more than $287,000. Erbe Favela had been meeting with Luz, posing as someone from the attorney general's office who could help her bribe the right security officials there to allow her cocaine shipments through the Mexico City airport, and he was reporting back everything that was said to the DEA.

But, as Luz's lawyer pointed out during her trial, Erbe Favela was himself a former-trafficker-turned-informant who had provided false information to the DEA before. None of the tips he passed on resulted in the seizure of any drugs or precursors owned by Luz. The man made a living selling information to the DEA, and he earned a tidy profit selling information to the agency about Luz. So it's any-one's guess how reliable his testimony was.

This is a problem with many cases built against traffickers. Pros-ecutors often rely on the accused's criminal cohorts as witnesses. It's something we see repeatedly in the US justice system. Most of those who testified against El Chapo during his high-profile trial in New York were former criminal associates of his, many of them deeply unsavory.

Luz's criminal lawyer, Feital, having overseen many cases for his drug trafficking clients, asked during her trial: Should the jury be prepared to take at their word the testimony of those who are also convicted narcos, who are hoping for reduced sentences in exchange for their cooperation, as well as being paid handsomely for their time?

In this case, the jury did find Luz guilty. Witness testimony, combined with government evidence—such as transcripts of her Blackberry messenger conversations and drug seizures of cocaine kilos stamped with the name JENCA (Luz's alleged nickname)—served as adequate evidence to jurors of her participation in the busi-ness. She was sentenced to twenty-two years in prison in July 2021. "Drug traffickers like Fajardo Campos tear at the very fabric of our communities. She made millions of dollars from pushing thousands of pounds of poison into American communities while at the same time fueling violence and crime across the United States. Today, justice was served," said Cheri Oz of the DEA's Phoenix Field Division at the time of Luz's sentencing.[12]

Feital took a different view. "Luz sacrificed herself by going to trial because of what happened to her children," he told me following her sentencing. "It was like a Greek tragedy."

THE STORY NEVER ENDS

I have no doubt there are dozens more of the kinds of women I have chosen to focus on in this book. Marllory, Digna, Sebastiana, Luz, Guadalupe, Yaneth, Emma, and Marixa are all women who had some visibility in the public sphere, whether due to the media coverage of their antics or court documents related to their legal processes in the United States. That information allowed me to build a narrative and an admittedly modest level of understanding about their involvement in their criminal enterprises. After I'd done the fieldwork in Mexico and Central America for this book, cases about women in the drug trade continued to emerge. Many of the names I had never heard mentioned before, but they were connected to well-known organizations.

YULI

About a year after I was in La Reforma, Guatemala, reporting on Marllory, Sebastiana, Yaneth, and the Lorenzana mafia, that part of the world sprang into the headlines. In April 2021, authorities made a major arrest in the small town of Usumatlán, a thirty-minute drive from where I had been doing research: they took Marta Julia Lorenzana-Cordon into custody, at the behest of the US government. Marta Julia, or Yuli, as she is best known (a Spanish-language pronunciation of Julia), is the sister of Eliu and Waldemar, and the daughter of Waldemar Lorenzana Lima (Waldemar Senior). Theirs was the drug trafficking mafia I described working with Marllory, Sebastiana, and Yaneth in chapter 3.

Photos of Yuli following her detention in May 2021 showed her sitting in a police truck, grinning, wearing layered white and blue shirts, as she clutched a bottle of water between her long white fingernails. She looked pretty relaxed for someone who had just been arrested, and there were some shots of her standing outside the police truck with her hands on her hips, chatting. But the language used in the indictment against her, which wasn't unsealed until six months after her detention, was strong. Yuli allegedly "played an integral, leadership role in the [drug trafficking] conspiracy," according to the charge sheet, which also claimed that the US government "has evidence personally implicating the Defendant in acts of violence, including murder."[1]

Yuli was a violent leader in what was once one of the most sophisticated and powerful drug trafficking organizations in the world, according to investigators.[2] I was stunned and a little horrified that, a couple of years into investigating women in the drug trade in Guatemala, I could have missed a key trafficking cog in the female machine. Reassuringly, my colleague Julie López felt similarly. She had worked with me on the research for chapter 3 and had long covered the Lorenzana drug trafficking clan. How had we completely missed Yuli's criminal evolution? Was she a secret powerhouse?

Turns out, she was.

I learned from those close to her that she was able to stay out of view because her trafficking networks were different from those of her brothers and her father. She worked with different suppliers in the region, so her name didn't emerge in the evidence that prosecutors gathered against her male family members. Gathering evidence to indict her took longer than it had taken to charge her brothers and father. This explained why she was absent from the transcripts and documents of the cases that revolved around her father and brothers, all of whom were eventually convicted before she was even indicted. The Lorenzana-Cordon family, I was told, was deeply dysfunctional and divided, with Yuli being significantly younger than her brothers.[3]

The indictment against her revealed that Yuli's drug trafficking networks were connected to another man, her husband, the notorious and feared trafficker Jairo Estuardo Orellana Morales. Her man, also known as "El Pelon," or "Baldy," because of his shaved head, started off in the drug trade working as a gunman for her family, as well as for other drug trafficking groups in the area. The couple likely got to know each other while he was working for her clan. Then, around 2008, Orellana Morales allegedly became the Guatemalan operator for the violent Mexican Zetas Cartel. This move suggests that he most likely broke ties with Yuli's family at that point, at least professionally, since the Lorenzana men worked with the Sinaloa Cartel, a rival group to the hyper-violent Zetas.

Orellana Morales was arrested in Zacapa in May 2014, at the behest of the DEA, following a firefight between his armed men and Guatemalan authorities. As the US investigation into Orellana Morales deepened, his wife, Yuli, came more clearly into view. Many of her contacts in the drug trade were also his, as noted by those close to her case. The evidence to indict her started to pile up. Orellana Morales was extradited to the US just over a year after his arrest. His case went quiet soon afterward, and his indictment remains under seal. It's fair to speculate that in the six-plus years he has been in the US justice system, he may have helped the government add to its collection of evidence on Yuli.

Which is all to say, Orellana Morales led the gringos to his wife, rather than the other way around.

HERLINDA

Southwest from where Yuli was arrested, on the coast of Honduras, another trafficking matriarch emerged as I was finishing this book.

Sixty-two-year-old Herlinda Bobadilla was detained in May 2022. She appeared incongruous in news agency photos. She cut a nonthreatening short, stout figure in a flower-print T-shirt, but she was flanked by heavily armed National Police dressed in black. Her wrists were tied together, and her features were obscured by a facemask as she was paraded in front of the Honduran press.

A $5 million bounty had been placed on Herlinda's head by the US government two weeks before her arrest. According to prosecutors, she oversaw the Montes drug trafficking network that operated from her family's base in the department of Colón, which used its fleet of planes, trucks, and boats to move cocaine via the coast from its partners in Colombia.

Herlinda was based on the eastern side of northern Honduras, and her organization worked "closely" with that of Digna Valle and her clan (the subject of chapter 1) as part of the cocaine highway that moved drugs from South America toward Mexico and the United States.[4] That cocaine then likely passed through the hands of Yuli's mafia in Guatemala, some of the male members of which worked with two of our protagonists: Marllory Chacón and Sebastiana Cottón. Finally, the cocaine moved into Mexico, where Guadalupe Fernández Valencia and Luz Irene Fajardo Campos had once been queens.

One of Herlinda's two sons, Tito Montes Bobadilla, was killed in the police operation that resulted in her detention. He was shot after he began firing at the police in a confrontation that ensued when the arrest raid began, according to the authorities. Her other son, Juan Carlos Montes Bobadilla, remains on the run.

The reports that emerged after Herlinda's arrest revealed more details about her life. She had been called in to help manage the Montes clan after its patriarch, García Montes, was killed in Colombia in 2004. She was the mother of six children with her husband—Alejandro Montes Alvarenga—and three of her kids also got into the game. As they were killed or captured, she took more and more control of the business. At the time of her arrest, according to the Honduran authorities, she was the owner of dozens of properties around her family's fiefdom in Colón.[5]

AN UPSIDE-DOWN WORLD

Both Yuli and Herlinda were invisible until their arrests and indictments. Without such documents, female protagonists in the drug war tend to remain more invisible than men. The drug trafficking world isn't like discovering new musicians or artists—you can't just go around asking what someone's up to and get a sense of it by hanging around. Doing so puts you in mortal danger.

We have, by now, circled back to the visibility, or invisibility, of these women in either the media or court paper trails, something that is affected by the male gaze. Who we see and hear about in this business is largely in the hands of law enforcement and the media, neither of which are objective observers. Who gets indicted? Who gets investigated? Who is deemed the bigger risk? All of these judgments play a massive role in deciding what gets covered and discussed. If women are perceived as being in the shadows of men and mere pawns in their game, then they're not considered worth investigating. But the stories of these patronas belie the idea that women's role in organized crime is minimal.

Most of the powerful women I've described in this book, perhaps with the exception of Marllory Chacón in Guatemala, had very low profiles or were completely unknown before they were arrested. Which begs the question: How many more are out there?

My understanding of the criminal underworld has been turned on its head. What I used to think was a man's world is increasingly appearing less so as I learn more about the women present in positions at every level of the drug trade. Now I question what we understand about organized crime and how it works. Fundamentally, how much can we know about the decision-making process and the dynamics within these organizations without understanding women's roles intimately? Their roles cannot be pigeonholed or oversimplified. Much as the women in today's licit, legal world are taking on more prominent roles and higher profiles, it's logical that such a trend should also be reflected in the criminal underworld. And in the case of the women in this book, they're all connected: by geography, by criminal organizations, and by shared business interests.

Marixa Lemus was a driving violent force on the Guatemala–El Salvador border, prepared to do anything to defeat her political nemesis.

Digna Valle, now in her sixties, helped bring down her entire trafficking clan and, possibly, a former president.

Luz Irene Fajardo Campos worked with her sons to traffic cocaine from Colombia and meth from Mexico, and she did so without a man by her side and without resorting to violence.

Sebastiana Cottón struck fear into the hearts of those who worked with her and went into battle with violent male rivals.

Marllory Chacón used her wits, looks, and education to build an empire described by the US government as one of the most prolific drug trafficking networks in Central America.

Yaneth Vergara Hernández had a criminal career spanning different generations in Colombia and Mexico. She worked with Colombia's most famous female trafficker, Griselda Blanco, as well as with Sebastiana Cottón and Marllory Chacón.

And Guadalupe Fernández Valencia operated in the high-ranking shadows alongside infamous and powerful men in the Sinaloa Cartel, including Joaquín "El Chapo" Guzmán and his sons.

I hope that throwing light on their criminal careers will help to dispel some of the myths and gender stereotypes about women in the drug cartels and create new narratives and conversations regarding las patronas of Latin America.

Meanwhile, the story of women in organized crime continues.

ACKNOWLEDGMENTS

The drive and dynamics behind this book started before I was a journalist, when I was a young tomboy who didn't conform to what was expected of me. I didn't want to wear dresses or makeup. I didn't want long hair. I showed no interest in dolls. I preferred writing to sewing or knitting, and I definitely didn't want to wear high-heeled shoes. As an adult and a journalist, I preferred covering crime and drugs to business and the advertising world where I started.

I've reneged on some of those commitments—I can manage the high heels now—but I still feel, acutely, that there are consequences for women who buck expectations, despite how far we have come. But the experience of resisting those expectations and the resulting judgment that followed as my life and career unfolded, and meeting the people I encountered along the way, brought me to write this book, which has been a hugely fulfilling experience.

The most important acknowledgment goes to the women—and men—who have let me into their lives to ask questions, and to follow them around and understand what they do. They are simply too many to mention, and some of them I met before I knew I was going to write this book. Some of them may not be alive to read it, others may not even care, but those conversations and the glimpses I got of their worlds had a huge impact on me and my understanding of organized crime. To Luz, Marllory, Sebastiana, Guadalupe, Marixa, Yaneth, Digna, and all of the other women whose cases I pulled apart and studied: I hope you can see the value in the exercise, despite the intrusion you might have felt.

I want to thank the individuals I've worked with at *VICE*. Global drugs editor Max Daly gave me a shot as a freelance writer and then recommended me as senior editor for Latin America when *VICE World News* was forged in the midst of the COVID pandemic. He replied to nearly every email and message when I was a freelancer, never dismissing my ideas, no matter how nutty they were, and he always had faith in my reporting. I owe a great debt to Katie Drummond, Erika Allen, and Michael Learmonth, my bosses and editors, for investing so much time in the *Patronas* series, which was based on the book, and published beforehand as a taster on *VICE*, with excellent editing by Tim Marchman and Leah Feiger. To Anna Merlan for showing me how to write to all of my women protagonists in US prisons, and to Juan Pablo Gallón Salazar for believing in the project and for helping get it out on VICE in Spanish.

Ramy Ghaly on *VICE*'s security team, along with Sharbil Nammour and Michael Buddle, held my hand virtually on innumerable reporting trips around the region for the fieldwork I did on this project in Mexico, Guatemala, Honduras, and El Salvador. I couldn't have done it without the support and confidence their virtual presence gave me. The team of reporters I worked with—Nathaniel Janowitz, Emily Green, Keegan Hamilton, and Luis Chaparro—continue to impress me every day and kept me grounded and enthused during the time I was researching and writing the book. Tips and help abounded, and no one at *VICE* griped when I took time off from editing to spend time reporting, which is still what I love most about this job. And thank you, Edgar Jaramillo at VICE Studios, for always having my back.

The team and managers at *InSight Crime*—including Jeremy McDermott and Steve Dudley—helped solidify my understanding of organized crime in the region and gave me invaluable experience in designing and managing long-term projects from inception to publication. Working with investigators, past and present, from all over the region taught me the value of collaboration, young blood, and friendship: Laura Ávila, Josefina Salomón, Felipe Puerta, Tristan Clavel, Parker Asmann, Héctor Silva Ávalos, and Juan Diego Posada are just some of those I had the honor to work with. *Narcas* was already taking form during the many field trips we made to some of the region's most unsavory places, reporting assignments that exemplified why I love journalism and research so much.

I will be forever indebted to my local colleagues, who worked with me in investigating and getting me as close as possible to so many of the women in this book and the stomping grounds they once ruled: Xiomara Orellana and Jorge Acosta in Honduras, Julie López and Fredy Contreras in Guatemala, Bryan Avelar in El Salvador and America Armenta in Sinaloa, Mexico.

I also owe a massive debt to all of the amazing women at the International Women's Media Fund (IWMF) who gave me a grant, which I added to the budget *VICE World News* also gave, to go forth and investigate this book idea when it was still all in my head. Special thanks to Mary Stucky, who has always believed in me and who rang me to ask me what I was working on when *Narcas* was formulating in my mind. That phone conversation turned into the game-changing grant. Massive thanks as well to Juanita Islas, who saw the process all the way through.

I also owe thanks to Romain Le Cour, and everyone at Noria, who included me in many conversations about the developing crime wars around Latin America. The Global Initiative Against Transnational Organized Crime (GITOC) has been a major supporter over the years, and I want to send a special thanks to Siria Gastélum, born and bred in Culiacán, Sinaloa, who has been an invaluable sounding board for so much of this work, especially the chapters on Mexico, and to Tuesday Reitano, for putting my skills to much use.

I have drawn both factually and spiritually from the work, enthusiasm, and attitude of historian Elaine Carey and academic Felia Allum, who started beating the drum of women in crime a lot sooner than I did. I will be forever grateful for the mini-mafia of women that we have formed investigating this issue.

I am lucky enough to have many friends who spent hours sitting around kitchen tables or strolling streets and mountains listening to me talk about Marllory, Sebastiana, Luz, and all of the other women in this book. Leslie Mazoch, Claudia Daut, Lisa McMunn, Julia Galiano-Rios, Will Grant, Ale Cuellar, Lisette Poole, Lexie Harrison-Cripps, Reed Johnson and Marla Dickerson, Zoe Smith, Rodrigo Román Alonso, Juan Sebastián Salamanca, Bonny Symons-Brown, and so many more: I lose track of the people who must be bored of hearing about *Narcas* by now, but I will be forever grateful for their power and willingness to listen and opine. A special thanks to my dear friend and one of the best journalists I've ever met, Jo Tuckman, who isn't around to read this book, but who I hope would have enjoyed it tremendously. The hours I was lucky enough to spend chatting with her about it and our lives on her Mexico City roof before cancer stole her away from us and her family will remain forever in my heart.

I owe a major thanks to Laura Dail, my tireless literary agent, who found and nurtured me and my ideas despite my slow pace and intermittent proposals. She never gave up on getting an idea out of me, and it took seven years between meeting and publishing for this book to happen.

Finally, I want to thank my family—my parents, Joe and Josette Bonello, for never turning away from me even when I deviated from the path that immigrant Maltese girls are supposed to take. To my younger sister Anthea, for always inspiring me, and to my brothers, Andrew and JP, for always having something to say that makes me laugh.

Lastly, I wouldn't be where I am without Ulises Escamilla Haro, who showed me a Mexico that changed my life forever, and who gave me Luca and Emiliano: my two shining lights who teach me something new every day and make all the hard work so worth it.

NOTES

INTRODUCTION

1. United States v. Fernandez Valencia, No. 09 CR 383–19 (N.D. Ill. E.D., August 24, 2021). The quotes come from the transcript of the sentencing hearing for the case.

2. *Fernandez Valencia*, 09 CR 383–19, August 24, 2021, sentencing hearing.

3. In Spain and in most Latin American countries, people have two surnames. The first is from their father's line, and the second is from their mother's line. When people are referred to only by a surname, it is the one they share with their father. Alfredillo is the diminutive form of Alfredo.

4. United States v. Guzman Loera et al., 09 CR 383 (N.D. Ill. E.D., April 23, 2015). The quotes come from the transcript of the ninth superseding indictment for the case.

5. Keegan Hamilton, "El Chapo's Wife Emma Coronel Turned Herself In," *VICE*, February 25, 2021, https://www.vice.com/en/article/qjp9px/el -chapos-wife-emma-coronel-turned-herself-in.

6. Coletta A. Youngers, Teresa García Castro, and Maria (Kiki) Manzur, *Women Behind Bars for Drug Offenses in Latin America: What the Numbers Make Clear*, Washington Office for Latin America, November 2020, https://www.wola .org/wp-content/uploads/2020/11/Final-Women-Behind-Bars-Report.pdf.

7. "Brenda," interview with the author in Pavón prison, Guatemala City, Guatemala, March 16, 2021. Her name has been changed to protect her identity, at her request.

8. Gloria, interview with the author in Pavón Prison, Guatemala City, Guatemala, March 16, 2021. Gloria asked that her second name not be used.

9. "Maria," interview with author in Tepito, Mexico City, November 2, 2021. Maria was the only name she gave.

10. Abel Jacobo Miller, interview with the author, May 22, 2021.

11. Jacobo Miller, interview, May 22, 2021.

12. Tessa, interview with the author, May 22, 2021. She asked that only her first name be used.

13. *Fernandez Valencia*, 09 CR 383–19, August 24, 2021, sentencing hearing.

14. Jelisa Castrodale, "El Chapo Smuggled Coke inside Fake Pickled Jalapeño Cans, Witness Testifies," *VICE*, November 28, 2018, https://www.vice .com/en/article/kzv339/witness-testifies-that-el-chapo-smuggled-coke-inside -fake-pickled-jalapeno-cans. Also, Alan Feuer, "7 Tons of Cocaine in Jalapeño Cans: The Evidence Against El Chapo," *New York Times*, April 10, 2018, https:// www.nytimes.com/2018/04/10/nyregion/prosecution-evidence-against-el -chapo.html.

15. Deborah Bonello, "Women Are Dying for the Narco Wife 'Buchona' Body," *VICE*, October 18, 2022, https://www.vice.com/en/article/3adjzw /mexico-buchona-plastic-surgery.

16. Anonymous former government official, interview with the author, Santa Rosa de Copán, Honduras, March 11, 2021. This former official asked not to be named.

17. Anonymous former government official, interview, March 11, 2021.

18. Mónica Ramírez Cano, phone interview with the author, January 20, 2020.

CHAPTER I: THE MATRIARCH

1. Juanita, interview with the author, March 9, 2021.

2. Anonymous former government official, interview with the author, Santa Rosa de Copán, Honduras, March 11, 2021.

3. Alex Papadovassilakis, "Cocaine Spike Puts Spotlight on Honduras Atlantic," *InSight Crime*, April 16, 2021, https://insightcrime.org/news/cocaine -spike-puts-spotlight-on-honduras-atlantic.

4. Emily Green, "Tigers, Giraffes, and Drug Lord Mansions: Welcome to Honduras' 'Narco State,'" *VICE World News*, July 7, 2022, https://www.vice .com/en/article/m7geaa/honduras-joya-grande-zoo-drug-lord-mansion.

5. Douglas Farah and Carl Meacham, *Alternative Governance in the Northern Triangle and Implications for U.S. Foreign Policy*, Center for Strategic and International Studies and Rowman and Littlefield, September 2015, 17–20, https://csis-website-prod.s3.amazonaws.com/s3fs-public/legacy_files/files /publication/150911_Farah_AlternativeGovernance_Web.pdf.

6. Farah and Meacham, *Alternative Governance*, 1.

7. Farah and Meacham, *Alternative Governance*, 7.

8. James Bosworth, "Honduras: Organized Crime Gaining Amid Political Crisis" Woodrow Wilson International Centre for Scholars, Latin American Program, December 2010, https://www.wilsoncenter.org/sites/default/files /media/documents/event/Bosworth.FIN.pdf.

9. Farah and Meacham, *Alternative Governance in the Northern Triangle and Implications for U.S. Foreign Policy*, 10 and 19.

10. Farah and Meacham, *Alternative Governance in the Northern Triangle and Implications for U.S. Foreign Policy*, 19.

11. The official municipal government website for the town of Florida, Copán, Honduras, welcomes visitors on behalf of Mayor Rember Cuestas. See https://portalunico.iaip.gob.hn/portal/index.php?portal=78.

12. "Teresa," interview with the author, March 11 2021.

13. Anonymous asylum seeker, telephone interview with the author, March 26, 2021. This asylum seeker, who was originally from El Espíritu, was in the US when I spoke with her.

14. Claudia Torrens, "Witness: 'El Chapo' Gave $1M to Honduran President's Brother," Associated Press, October 7, 2019.

15. Anonymous asylum seeker, interview, March 26, 2021.

16. Torrens, "Witness."

17. Deborah Bonello, "Former Honduran President Just Got Arrested on Cocaine Trafficking Charges," *VICE World News*, February 15, 2022, https://www.vice.com/en/article/xgd5gq/honduras-president-juan-orlando-hernandez-arrested-drug-charges.

18. Mike Vigil, interview with the author, April 12, 2020.

19. Santos Rodríguez Orellana, interview with the author, April 2020.

CHAPTER 2: NARCO WOMEN—THE STORY SO FAR

1. Elaine Carey, interview with the author, December 7, 2021.

2. Elaine Carey, *Women Drug Traffickers: Mules, Bosses, and Organized Crime* (Albuquerque: University of New Mexico Press, 2014).

3. Carey, interview, December 7, 2021.

4. Dennis Rodgers, interview with the author, January 21, 2022. Rodgers is a research professor at the Department of Anthropology and Sociology at the Graduate Institute of International and Development Studies in Geneva and has studied gangs extensively in Latin America and Asia.

5. Rodgers, interview, January 21, 2022.

6. Rodgers, interview, January 21, 2022.

7. Felia Allum, interview with the author, August 25, 2021.

8. Allum, interview, August 25, 2021.

9. Felia Allum and Irene Marchi, "Analyzing the Role of Women in Italian Mafias: The Case of the Neapolitan Camorra," *Qualitative Sociology* 41, no. 3 (August 2018): 361–80, https://link.springer.com/article/10.1007/s11133-018-9389-8.

10. Allum and Marchi, "Analyzing the Role of Women in Italian Mafias."

11. An anonymous experienced female prosecutor in the US, interview with the author, November 2021.

12. Elaine Carey, interview with the author, December 7, 2021.

13. US criminal lawyer, interview with the author, March 8, 2021. This lawyer asked not to be named.

14. Bonnie Klapper, interview with the author, November 24, 2021.

15. Douglas Farah, interview with the author, January 13, 2022. All the Farah quotes are from this interview.

16. James Brooke, "A Drug Lord Is Buried as a Folk Hero," *New York Times*, December 4, 1993, https://www.nytimes.com/1993/12/04/world/a-drug-lord-is-buried-as-a-folk-hero.html.

17. Mo Hume, interview with the author, January 13, 2022. Hume is a professor of Latin American politics at the University of Glasgow.

18. Elaine Carey, "'Selling Is More of a Habit than Using': Narcotraficante Lola la Chata and Her Threat to Civilization, 1930–1960," *Journal of*

Women's History 21, no. 2 (Summer 2009): 62–89, https://history.msu.edu/files
/2010/04/Elaine-Carey2.pdf.

19. Carey, *Women Drug Traffickers*, chapter 4.

20. Carey, *Women Drug Traffickers*, chapter 4.

21. Carey, "'Selling Is More of a Habit.'"

22. Carey, "'Selling Is More of a Habit.'"

23. Carey, "'Selling Is More of a Habit.'"

24. Elaine Carey and José Carlos Cisneros Guzmán, "The Daughters of La Nacha: Profiles of Women Traffickers," *NACLA Report on the Americas*, May/June 2011, https://nacla.org/sites/default/files/A04403025_8.pdf.

25. Carey, *Women Drug Traffickers*, 381–400.

26. "No Antiwoman Job Bias in the Narcotics Trade," *New York Times*, April 22, 1975, https://www.nytimes.com/1975/04/22/archives/no-antiwoman-job-bias-in-the-narcotics-trade.html.

27. "No Antiwoman Job Bias," *New York Times*.

28. Peter Axthelm and Anthony Marrow, "The Drug Vigilantes," *Newsweek*, April 16, 1976, quoted in Carey, *Women Drug Traffickers*, chapter 5.

29. Carey, *Women Drug Traffickers*, chapter 5.

30. Alan Feuer, "El Chapo 'Tried to Kill Me': A Final Witness Confronts the Drug Lord," *New York Times*, July 17, 2019, https://www.nytimes.com /2019/07/17/nyregion/el-chapo-andrea-velez.html.

31. Carey, *Women Drug Traffickers*, chapter 5.

32. Deborah Bonello, "Mexico's Most Famous Female Narco Just Got a New Gig: TikTok Influencer," *VICE World News*, July 22, 2022, https://www .vice.com/en/article/wxnd7m/mexico-female-narco-tiktok-influencer.

33. Jo Tuckman, "Queen of the Pacific Has Mexico Hooked as She Faces Drug Charges," *Guardian*, October 6, 2007, https://www.theguardian.com /world/2007/oct/06/mexico.

34. Congressional Research Services, *Mexico's Drug Cartels*, February 25, 2008, https://www.everycrsreport.com/files/20080225_RL34215_6d89146a5 fcd867022970d473876f7648f0f2511.pdf.

35. Kyra Gurney, "'Narco-Mom' Takes Charge of Tijuana Cartel," *InSight Crime*, June 26, 2014. https://insightcrime.org/news/brief/narco-mom-takes -charge-of-tijuana-cartel/.

36. Gurney, "'Narco-Mom' Takes Charge."

CHAPTER 3: BETRAYAL WITHIN A FEMALE TRAFFICKING THREESOME

1. Yaneth Del Carmen Vergara Hernández, email to the author, 2021. After her initial written response, Vergara Hernández and I corresponded via CorrLinks email service, which is available for communicating with people incarcerated in US federal prisons, during 2021 and 2022.

2. Vergara Hernández, email to the author, 2021.

3. United States v. Henry de Jesus Lopez Londono, No. 10-20763-CR-Graham, 2018 US Dist., (S.D. Cal., February 27, 2018). This exchange is taken from the court transcript.

4. U.S. Department of the Treasury, "Treasury Sanctions Los Urabenos Leadership," July 23, 2014, https://home.treasury.gov/news/press-releases /jl2577#:~:text=Los%20Urabenos%20is%20the%20largest,group)%20 currently%20operating%20in%20Colombia.

5. US Attorney General's Office, "Colombian Drug Kingpin Sentenced to 31 Years in Prison for Drug Trafficking," June 19, 2018, https://www.justice .gov/usao-sdfl/pr/colombian-drug-kingpin-sentenced-31-years-prison-drug -trafficking.

6. US Department of Justice, "Leader of Guatemalan Drug Trafficking Organization Sentenced to Life in Prison," February 22, 2018, https://www .justice.gov/opa/pr/leader-guatemalan-drug-trafficking-organization-sentenced -life-prison.

7. United States v. Eliu Elixander Lorenzana-Cordon and Waldemar Lorenzana-Cordon, No. 1:03-cr-00331-CKK (D.C. Cir. 2016). This conversation is taken from a transcript of court events on March 14, 2016.

8. *Lorenzana-Cordon and Lorenzana-Cordon*, 1:03-cr-00331-CKK, March 14, 2016.

9. US Department of the Treasury, "Treasury Targets Top Guatemalan Drug Trafficker," January 19, 2012, https://home.treasury.gov/news/press -releases/tg1395.

10. Steve Fraga, phone interview with the author, August 3, 2021.

11. "Juan," interview with the author, Zacapa, Guatemala, March 13, 2021. Juan's name has been changed to protect his identity.

12. "Juan," interview, March 13, 2021.

13. Hugo Alvarado and Byron Vásquez, "Marllory Chacón Busca Salir de Lista Negra," *Prensa Libre*, May 23, 2014, https://www.prensalibre.com /guatemala/justicia/marllory-chacon-capturada-se-encuentra-ee-uu-o -1142885889.

14. Steven Dudley, "Guatemala's Mafia State and the Case of Mauricio López Bonilla," *InSight Crime*, December 15, 2016, https://insightcrime.org /investigations/guatemala-mafia-state-case-of-lopez-bonilla.

15. US Department of the Treasury, "Treasury Targets Top Guatemalan Drug Trafficker."

16. "Apoyo Multitudinario a los Lorenzana," *Prensa Libre*, July 25, 2009, video, 0:14/2:07, https://www.youtube.com/watch?v=oNfoPTp8ZzM.

17. *Lorenzana-Cordon and Lorenzana-Cordon*, 1:03-cr-00331-CKK, March 8, 2016. Sebastiana's descriptions in this chapter of the incident at Don Walde's home in La Reforma and the aftermath of that meeting are taken from a transcript of court events for this case.

18. *Doña* is a respectful way to address a woman, and *Tana* is a nickname for Sebastiana.

19. Deborah Bonello, "How a Single Mom Became the Boss of Guatemala's Drug Lords," *VICE World News*, October 26, 2021, https://www.vice .com/en/article/88nzj5/guatemala-drug-lord-bosses-cotton-vasquez-chacon -rossell.

20. United States v. Sebastiana Hortencia Cotton Vasquez and Oliverio Fernando Paleaz Solano, No. 1:14-CR-20557-MGC-1m (D.C. Fla. S.D., October 14, 2015). Sebastiana's descriptions here are excerpts from the transcript of her sentencing hearing.

21. Anonymous criminal rival of Sebastiana Cottón Vásquez, interview with the author, Guatemala City, March 17, 2021.

22. *Cotton Vasquez and Paleaz Solano*, 1:14-CR-20557-MGC-1m, October 14, 2015. From the transcript of the sentencing hearing.

23. "Sebastiana Hortencia Cottón Vásquez 'Doña Tana,'" Personas de Interes (2014), OCCRP Aleph, https://aleph.occrp.org/entities/26447253d631 ec29fcc73d458cfb1f4f9c05cd9f.5d7415800a0b39fa84e118df831b00421d 8275c0. OCCRP Aleph is a global archive of research material for investigative reporting.

24. US Department of Justice, "Leader of Guatemalan Drug Trafficking."

25. *Cotton Vasquez and Paleaz Solano*, 1:14-CR-20557-MGC-1m, October 14, 2015. From the transcript of the sentencing hearing.

26. *Cotton Vasquez and Paleaz Solano*, 1:14-CR-20557-MGC-1m, October 14, 2015.

27. *Cotton Vasquez and Paleaz Solano*, 1:14-CR-20557-MGC-1m, October 14, 2015.

28. United States v. Yaneth Del Carmen Vergara Hernandez, No.14–20557-cr-Cooke (D.C. Fla. S.D.).

29. David Gagne and Steven Dudley, "Following Sentence, Intrigue around Guatemala's 'Queen' Turns Political," *InSight Crime*, May 7, 2015, https://insight crime.org/news/analysis/guatemala-drug-trafficking-queen-sentenced-in-us-court.

30. Bonello, "How a Single Mom Became the Boss."

31. Ministry of Justice and Law, Colombia, Executive resolution number 072, 2015 [*Resolución ejecutiva número 072 de 2015, por la cual se decide sobre una solicitud de extradición*], May 11, 2015. This resolution is a decision about an extradition request.

32. Anonymous criminal rival of Sebastiana, interview, March 17, 2021.

CHAPTER 4: THE WOMEN OF THE MARA SALVATRUCHA

1. Isabel, interview with the author, November 16, 2021.

2. Steven Dudley, Héctor Silva Ávalos, and Juan José Martínez, *MS13 in the Americas: How the World's Most Notorious Gang Defies Logic, Resists Destruction* (Washington, DC: InSight Crime and the Center for Latin American and Latino Studies, American University, 2018), 3, https://insightcrime.org/wp -content/uploads/2018/02/MS13-in-the-Americas-InSight-Crime-English-3.pdf.

3. Dudley, Silva Ávalos, and Martínez, *MS13 in the Americas*, 15.

4. David Gagne, "InSight Crime's 2016 Homicide Round-Up," *Insight Crime*, January 16, 2017, https://insightcrime.org/news/analysis/insight-crime -2016-homicide-round-up.

5. Elijah Stevens, "El Salvador Attorney General: Two-Thirds of Homicides Gang-Related," *InSight Crime*, December 2, 2015, https://insightcrime

.org/news/brief/el-salvador-attorney-general-two-thirds-of-homicides-gang
-related/.

6. Sonja Wolf, email exchange with the author, December 2021.

7. Deborah Bonello, "Women in Guatemala: The New Faces of Extortion?," *InSight Crime*, April 26, 2019, https://insightcrime.org/investigations
/women-guatemala-new-faces-extortion-2.

8. Marcela Gereda, Carolina Escobar Sarti, José Manuel Ramírez, and Misael Castro, *Violentas y Violentadas Relaciones de Género en las Maras Salvatrucha y Barrio 18 del Triángulo Norte de Centroamérica* (Geneva: Interpeace, 2013), https://idl-bnc-idrc.dspacedirect.org/bitstream/handle/10625/50910/IDL
-50910.pdf.

9. Jamie Stockwell, "In MS-13, a Culture of Brutality and Begging," *Washington Post*, May 2, 2005, https://www.washingtonpost.com/archive/politics
/2005/05/02/in-ms-13-a-culture-of-brutality-and-begging/757a75a7-d408
-44d5-91e6-80881c490dcd.

10. Stockwell, "In MS-13, a Culture of Brutality."

11. Terry Frieden, "Two Convicted, Two Acquitted in Suburban Virginia Street Gang Trial," CNN.com, May 17, 2005, https://edition.cnn.com/2005
/LAW/05/17/ms13.trial.verdicts/index.html.

12. Daniel Schorn, "The Fight Against MS-13," *60 Minutes*, CBS News, December 1, 2005, https://www.cbsnews.com/news/the-fight-against-ms-13.

13. Samuel Logan, *This Is for the Mara Salvatrucha: Inside the MS-13, America's Most Violent Gang* (New York: Hyperion, July 2009); Samuel Logan, "This Is for the Mara Salvatrucha: Inside the MS-13, America's Most Violent Gang," *Immigration Daily*, August 24, 2009, https://ilw.com/articles/2009,0824
-logan.shtm.

14. Juan José Martínez, interview with the author, November 2021. Martínez has documented El Salvador's street gangs for decades. I also interviewed another expert who is a former members of MS-13, who asked not to be named, via phone, December 7, 2021.

15. Martínez, interview, November 2021.

16. Dudley, Silva Ávalos, and Martínez, *MS13 in the Americas*, 26.

17. Dudley, Silva Ávalos, and Martínez, *MS13 in the Americas*, 26.

18. Juan Martínez d'Aubuisson, "Así Viven y Mueren las Mujeres Pandilleras en El Salvador," *Factum*, March 11, 2016, https://www.revistafactum.com
/asi-viven-y-mueren-las-mujeres-pandilleras-en-el-salvador.

19. Martínez d'Aubuisson, "Así Viven y Mueren las Mujeres Pandilleras."

20. Martínez d'Aubuisson, "Así Viven y Mueren las Mujeres Pandilleras."

21. US Institute of Diplomacy and Human Rights (USIDHR), "Tackling Violence Against Women in the Northern Triangle of Central America (NTCA)," November 14, 2021, https://usidhr.org/violence-against-women.

22. USIDHR, "Tackling Violence."

23. "Adriana," interview with the author, November 18, 2021. I spoke with Adriana in San Salvador, El Salvador. Her name has been changed to protect her identity.

24. "Juan," interview with the author, November 18, 2021. I spoke with Juan in San Salvador, El Salvador. His name has been changed to protect his identity.

25. El Salvador Attorney General documents outlining witness testimony and seized evidence related to the case of Esmeralda and her criminal cohorts, accessed at their headquarters in San Salvador, El Salvador, November 2021.

26. Martínez, interview, November 2021.

27. Sonja Wolf, email exchange with the author, December 2021.

28. Wolf, email exchange, December 2021.

29. Wolf, email exchange, December 2021.

30. Wolf, email exchange, December 2021.

31. El Salvador Attorney General documents, accessed at their headquarters in San Salvador, El Salvador, November 2021.

32. El Salvador Attorney General documents, accessed November 2021.

33. El Salvador Attorney General documents, accessed November 2021.

34. World Bank Group, "Poverty and Equity Brief, Latin America & the Caribbean: El Salvador," April 2021, https://databank.worldbank.org/data /download/poverty/987B9C90-CB9F-4D93-AE8C-750588BF00QA/AM2020 /Global_POVEQ_SLV.pdf.

35. El Salvador Attorney General documents, November 2021.

36. El Salvador Attorney General documents, November 2021.

CHAPTER 5: THE LEMUS SISTERS AND THE BATTLE FOR MOYUTA

1. Coletta A. Youngers, Teresa García Castro, and Maria (Kiki) Manzur, *Women Behind Bars for Drug Offenses in Latin America: What the Numbers Make Clear* (Washington, DC: WOLA, 2020), 6–8, https://www.wola.org/wp-content /uploads/2020/11/Final-Women-Behind-Bars-Report.pdf.

2. Youngers, García Castro, and Manzur, *Women Behind Bars for Drug Offenses in Latin America*, 9.

3. Youngers, García Castro, and Manzur, *Women Behind Bars for Drug Offenses in Latin America*, 6; 10–14.

4. Local residents in Ciudad Pedro de Alvarado, Moyuta, Guatemala, interview with the author, March 2021. Those whom I spoke to asked not to be named for security reasons. Also, Guatemala's anti-narcotics prosecutor at the time, Gerson Alegría, confirmed this information during an interview with the author in Guatemala City on March 18, 2021. I also talked with these residents about what happened at the Hotel Los Cuernos.

5. Alex Papadovassilakis and Héctor Silva Ávelos, "A Mayor and a Wave of Narco Violence on Guatemala's Pacific, *"InSight Crime,* January 29, 2021, https://insightcrime.org/investigations/mayor-narco-violence-guatemala -pacific.

6. Ministerio Público, Guatemala, "Presuntos Secuestradores Capturados," April 16, 2014, https://www.mp.gob.gt/noticia/presuntos-secuestradores -capturados.

7. Ministerio Público, Guatemala, "Presuntos Secuestradores," April 16 2014.

8. Gerson Alegría, interview with the author, March 18, 2021, Guatemala City.

9. Roberto Marroquín Fuentes, interview with the author via Zoom, August 30, 2021.

10. Jimmy Morales, then president of Guatemala, posted a tweet May 26, 2017: "Thanks to the efficient coordination of [the security forces], Marixa Lemus 'La Patrona' has been captured." Translated by the author from original Spanish: "Gracias a la eficiente coordinación entre los equipos de Mingob, PNC y autoridades de El Salvador, se captura a Marixa Lemus 'La Patrona'": https://twitter.com/jimmymoralesgt/status/867803548851077120.

11. Miguel Barrientos, "Hermano del Alcalde de Moyuta es Capturado en El Salvador por Narcotráfico," *Prensa Libre*, May 31, 2017, https://www.prensalibre.com/guatemala/justicia/hermano-del-alcalde-moyuta-es-capturado-en-el-salvador-por-narcotrafico.

12. Alan Ajiatas, interview with the author, March 18, 2021, Guatemala City.

CHAPTER 6: SINALOA, AND EMMA CORONEL'S BEGINNING, MIDDLE, AND END

1. Natalia Reyes, interview with the author, March 20, 2022.

2. Anabel Hernandez, "Murder, Torture, Drugs: Cartel Kingpin's Wife Says That's Not the 'El Chapo' She Knows," *Los Angeles Times*, February 21, 2016. https://www.latimes.com/world/mexico-americas/la-fg-el-chapo-wife-20160221-story.html.

3. Tom Phillips, "Mexican President Ignores Coronavirus Restrictions to Greet El Chapo's Mother," *Guardian*, March 30, 2020, https://www.theguardian.com/world/2020/mar/30/andres-manuel-lopez-obrador-el-chapo-mother-mexico.

4. Sara Bruna Quiñónez Estrada, interview with the author, February 2022. Quiñónez Estrada is Sinaloa's attorney general.

5. Janet Martínez Quintero, interview with author, Sinaloa, Mexico, February 28, 2022.

6. Brenda, interview with the author, Sinaloa, Mexico, February 28, 2022. Brenda asked me not to use her surname.

7. María Teresa Guerra Ochoa, interview with the author in Sinaloa, Mexico, February 19, 2022. Guerra Ochoa is head of the state women's ministry.

8. Dr. Rafaela Martínez Terrazas, interview with the author, Sinaloa, Mexico, February 22, 2022.

9. Deborah Bonello, "Women Are Dying for the Narco Wife 'Buchona' Body," *VICE*, October 18, 2022, https://www.vice.com/en/article/3adjzw/mexico-buchona-plastic-surgery.

10. "Muere Mujer en Culiacán tras Hacerse Mini-lipo; Había Entrado a Una Cundina [A Woman Dies in Culiacán After Getting a Mini-lipo Treatment; She Was Part of a Pyramid Scheme]," *El Sol De Sinaloa*, March 4, 2022, https://www.elsoldesinaloa.com.mx/policiaca/muere-mujer-en-culiacan-tras-hacerse-mini-lipo-habia-entrado-a-una-cundina-7945535.html. Article title translated by the author.

11. Bonello, "Women Are Dying."

12. Michael Daly, "She Was the Cartel's Top Assassin. And Then Her Boyfriend Turned Her In," *Daily Beast*, April 14, 2017, https://www.thedailybeast.com/she-was-the-cartels-top-assassin-and-then-her-boyfriend-turned-her-in.

13. "Adolescente de 15 Años se Mata en Sinaloa con Subametralladora al Grabar Video en TikTok" [15-Year-Old Adolescent Kills Herself in Sinaloa with a Submachine Gun as She Recorded a Video for TikTok]," *Revista Proceso*, January 28, 2022, https://www.proceso.com.mx/nacional/2022/1/28/adolescente-de-15-anos-se-mata-en-sinaloa-con-subametralladora-al-grabar-video-en-tiktok-279981.html.

14. Siria Gastélum interview with the author, February 25, 2022.

15. Quiñónez Estrada, interview, February 2022.

16. Anonymous local resident, interview with the author, Sinaloa, Mexico, February 2022. The resident asked not to be named.

17. Emily Saul and Ruth Brown, "El Chapo's Wife Laughs as His Mistress Weeps on the Stand," *New York Post*, January 17, 2019, https://nypost.com/2019/01/17/el-chapos-wife-laughs-as-his-mistress-cries-on-the-stand.

18. Mike Vigil, interview with the author, July 2019. Vigil was the chief of DEA international operations in Mexico for thirteen years.

19. Bonnie Klapper, interview with the author, January 29, 2022.

20. Keegan Hamilton, "El Chapo's Wife Emma Coronel Turned Herself In," *VICE News*, February 25, 2021, https://www.vice.com/en/article/qjp9px/el-chapos-wife-emma-coronel-turned-herself-in.

21. María Isabel Cruz Bernal, interview with the author, February 18, 2022.

22. United Nations Office of the High Commissioner for Human Rights, "Press Conference Following the Visit of the Committee on Enforced Disappearances to Mexico," November 26, 2021, https://www.ohchr.org/en/statements/2021/11/press-conference-following-visit-committee-enforced-disappearances-mexico.

23. Micaela Varela, "La Administración de López Obrador Acumula Más de 21.500 Personas Desaparecidas [The Administration of López Obrador Accumulates 21,500 Missing People]," *El País*, July 8, 2021, https://elpais.com/mexico/2021-07-08/la-administracion-de-lopez-obrador-acumula-mas-de-21500-personas-desaparecidas.html. Title translated by the author.

24. Mirtha Mendoza, interview with the author, Sinaloa, Mexico, February 26, 2022.

25. Abel Jacobo Miller, interview with the author, May 22, 2021.

26. Maria Lopez, interview with the author, May 2021. Maria Lopez is a pseudonym.

27. Kathleen, interview with the author, Sinaloa, Mexico, May 22, 2021. She asked not to use her second name.

28. Ana Jacobo, interview with the author, Sinaloa, Mexico, May 2021.

CHAPTER 7: THE FEMALE CHAPO

1. United States v. Luz Irene Fajardo Campos, No. 1:16-cr-00154-KBJ (D.C. Cir. 2021). My account of the abduction of the Avilés Fajardo brothers

is based on what was said by Luz Fajardo Campos's criminal lawyer and by Luz herself during the closing statements before her sentencing on July 27, 2021, as recorded in the court transcript for this case. It also draws from my interview with Fajardo Campos's father, Ignacio Fajardo Arroyo, in Culiacán, Sinaloa, on May 25, 2021. Fajardo Campos had at least three sons who worked with her in the drug trafficking business: Eduardo Luis Avilés Fajardo, Francisco Ruben Avilés Fajardo, and Sixto Benerando Avilés Fajardo, according to court documents. It's not clear which two out of those three sons were murdered that day on the highway.

2. *Fajardo Campos*, 1:16-cr-00154-KBJ, December 12, 2019, jury trial.

3. Deborah Bonello, "This Woman Ran Her Own Mexican Drug Cartel—and It Ended Very Badly," *VICE World News*, July 29, 2021, https://www.vice.com/en/article/y3deg7/this-woman-ran-her-own-mexican-drug-cartel-and-it-ended-very-badly.

4. *Fajardo Campos*, 1:16-cr-00154-KBJ, July 27, 2021, sentencing hearing.

5. *Fajardo Campos*, 1:16-cr-00154-KBJ, July 27, 2021, sentencing hearing.

6. *Fajardo Campos*, 1:16-cr-00154-KBJ, July 27, 2021. Judge John D. Bates during the sentencing hearing. Taken from the court transcript.

7. Keegan Hamilton, "El Chapo's Son Was Just Captured—Then Freed After the Cartel Attacked," *VICE News*, October 17, 2019, https://www.vice.com/en/article/vb5q3y/confirmed-el-chapos-son-captured-amid-gun-fights-and-chaos-in-sinaloa-mexico.

8. At the time that this book was nearing completion, eight journalists were killed in Mexico in the first six months of 2022 alone, a sad trend that the country has seen over decades. The Committee for Protection of Journalists (CPJ) and other nonprofits provide the most up-to-date information about this violence against journalists in Mexico. Visit https://cpj.org/americas/mexico/ for more information.

9. Ignacio Fajardo Arroyo, interview with the author, Culiacán, Sinaloa, Mexico, May 25, 2021.

10. *Fajardo Campos*, 1:16-cr-00154-KBJ. December 16, 2019, jury trial.

11. *Fajardo Campos*, 1:16-cr-00154-KBJ, December 12, 2019, jury trial.

12. US Department of Justice, "Leader of a Sophisticated Drug Trafficking Organization and Prolific Ally of the Sinaloa Cartel Sentenced," July 27, 2021, https://www.justice.gov/opa/pr/leader-sophisticated-drug-trafficking-organization-and-prolific-ally-sinaloa-cartel-sentenced.

CONCLUSION

1. United States v. Marta Julia Lorenzana-Cordon, (D.C. Cir. 2019), Case 1:20-cr-00133-CKK. Indictment document dated December 6, 2019.

2. US Department of Justice, "Leader of Guatemalan Drug Trafficking Organization Sentenced to Life in Prison," May 10, 2018, https://www.justice.gov/opa/pr/leader-guatemalan-drug-trafficking-organization-sentenced-life-prison-0.

3. Anonymous former DEA agent, phone interview with author, February 15, 2022. This agent worked on the Marta Julia Lorenzana-Cordon case.

4. US Department of Justice, "Former Leader of Honduran Cocaine Trafficking Organization Sentenced to 37 Years in Prison," April 5, 2019, https://www.justice.gov/opa/pr/former-leader-honduran-cocaine-trafficking -organization-sentenced-37-years-prison.

5. BBC News Mundo, "Quién es Herlinda Bobadilla 'la Chinda,' la Poderosa Líder del Clan Montes Bobadilla Arrestada en Honduras," May 16, 2022, https://www.bbc.com/mundo/noticias-america-latina-61468942.

INDEX

and, 142; Cachiros and, 25;
Catholic church and, 18; cocaine
trafficking, 16–17, 23–25, 28, 56;
Cottón and, 63; Digna's brothers,
21; rapes, 27; Sinaloa Cartel and,
25. *See also* El Espíritu
Vélez, Andrea, 47–48
Vergara Hernández, Yaneth: in
Aliceville federal prison, 52–53;
Chacón Rossell and, 91, 140;
cocaine trafficking, 55, 144;
court testimony, 54; June 2013
meeting, 51, 63–64; prison term,
65–66
VICE World News, 27, 35, 52
Vigil, Mike, 31, 117

Washington Post, 72
weapons trafficking, 7, 45, 57

wives or girlfriends, 4, 36, 47–48,
87–88, 107. *See also* buchonas;
Coronel, Emma; Ochoa Félix,
Claudia; plastic surgery
Wolf, Sonja, 71, 81
women's role: criminal intent and,
39–40; drug trade leadership,
42–43; incarceration, 89–90;
low profiles of, 143; matriarchal
dynamic, 45, 48; poverty and
motivation, 90–91; victims, 3, 5,
36, 38. *See also* Coronel, Emma;
gangs, women's role

Zacapa, Guatemala, 56–59, 141
Zambada, Ismael "El Mayo," 12,
116, 130
Zelaya, Manuel, 25
Zetas Cartel, 141